To Tom

Robert J. Burger

A Guide to Successful Planting

by

Robert J. Burger

DORRANCE PUBLISHING CO., INC.
PITTSBURGH, PENNSYLVANIA 15222

ISBN # 0-8059-3286-0
Printed in the United States of America

First Printing

Contents

I am the author. I think you, the reader, might like to know more about me. Due to the death of my mother when I was six I came to be part of the Corcoran family in Marion, New York. I was married at age 26 in 1939. My wife and I raised two sons and five daughters. After Will Corcoran died I was forced, due to his debts, to sell the farm. I obtained employment with a conveyor installation company from Detroit which was installing anti-aircraft shell conveyors at General Railway Signal in Rochester. Upon completion of that system I remained with the company to help maintain it. While with the company I apprenticed as a millwright. I also purchased the land that was to become my nursery. After the war I joined Fasco Industries, also a Rochester firm, first as millwright, then advancing to maintenance assistant and finally to supervisor of maintenance. While with them I began my nursery with the intent of growing cut Christmas trees. The first planting was 2000 Colorado Blue Spruce. As they began to gain size a friend suggested I might sell them for landscaping homes. I began to do so to discover it was rewarding in new friendships, in an inner satisfaction that seemed to be slipping away at Fasco, so I quit Fasco to give full attention to growing bushes and trees. I learned much and it is that knowledge I am passing on to you. So I offer you forty years of experience in the growing of trees and bushes.

I have tried in this book to convey information about the growing of trees and bushes that I have learned during the past forty years as a nurseryman. I have tried to write it in a manner that reflects the relationship that I've had and the large number of people who have been my customers these many years. The questions asked of me caused me to study extensively, to experiment, to draw conclusions. I have learned much. It is that knowledge I am passing on to you.

The picture of me at my typewriter is with two novels that Dorrance has published for me. I also have a new type of signal for rural mailboxes that the Postal Department has approved. I have contacted producing companies. Please wish me luck in my endeavors.

My Credentials

I have owned and operated a plant nursery for forty years. The word "plant" is used to describe the growing of both trees and bushes. At one time in life I had 23,000 plants growing. They varied in size and in variety. My purpose in this book is to pass on to others the many facts I have learned.

My nursery came to me accidently. I had purchased land without intending to farm it, as I was employed in a business several miles away. What to do with the land? Leave it idle? My decision to plant part to evergreens, with the thought in mind of producing cut Christmas trees, led me to scan booklets advertising seedlings. The caption accompanying the Colorado Blue Spruce, The Queen of the Christmas Tree, captured my attention. Consequently I purchased my first 2,000 seedlings.

Several years passed and the trees had reached a two to three foot size with the variations of color which are characteristic of that variety. A friend came to see the fascinating colors and his chance remark, "you could sell these to home owners for landscaping," gave me the idea of doing just that. They did sell, and for several more years I spent part of spring and autumn going from door to door in new housing areas to sell my beautiful trees. Many of those I met asked to come to my fledgling nursery to personally select trees, and in the end I was forced to give up my selling on the road. I began to plant deciduous trees and bushes, as well as other evergreen varieties; each new variety was a new challenge. I studied much and I learned much. Many of the things I learned are not easily found in books. That is the reason for this one.

I wish to thank all the hundreds of people who have purchased from my nursery. Almost all have remained my friends. It is time to wind down from the hard physical work. I still love trees and, what is more, I love people who love trees. Perhaps, together, you and I can relive that pleasure—I by offering advice and you benefitting from that advice. In the meantime, happy tree planting, dear friends.

Spruce Trees

There are many varieties of evergreens. Many are not suitable for landscaping purposes. In the recognized varieties that are suitable are certain spruces, firs, and pines. Hemlock is also used; it is a member of the pine family.

This section of the book will concentrate on spruces. It will explain fully all that is required to grow beautiful trees. Among the spruces, the Colorado Blue is considered one of the most valuable ones in landscaping. It is slow growing with a range of coloring that can vary from dark green to silvery blue. It is very hardy, surviving very low temperatures and the thrust of strong winds without noticeable effect. It grows best in a well-drained, rich-textured soil.

Additional spruces that will be described are Norway, White, Black Hills, and Englemann.

Small evergreen trees are called seedlings. Seedlings are grown from seed produced by cones. The cone petals open in late autumn to scatter the seeds to the ground, where they lay dormant through the winter. In the spring, if conditions are favorable, they sprout and begin to grow. Cones that fall to the ground during windstorms in late autumn generally have dislodged seed before falling. Cones can be used as campfire material, as decorative items in Christmas wreaths, and in other ways.

Evergreens are often spoken of as friendly trees. They stand in lawns night and day giving silent greeting to those who enter and leave. They protect deer on cold nights in wooded areas by providing shelter from wind and snow. They are the favorite nesting places of robins. They mute vehicle noise from roadways, offer protection from prevailing winds, and give privacy if desired. To know them better is to love them. This is my wish for you.

Seedlings in beds growing at Carino Nurseries, Pennsylvania.

Evergreen Seedlings

Very small evergreen trees are called seedlings. They are grown in nurseries that sell only at small size. Nurseries such as mine buy seedlings with the intent of growing them to larger sizes for sale either to wholesale or retail customers. Most are resold before reaching eight feet in height, but there are nurseries that specialize in the growing and replanting of much larger trees. Larger trees have more extensive root systems and more has to be severed in digging such trees. Root pruning large trees gives them a better chance of survival. Root pruning is the cutting off of main roots far enough in advance of the removal date to force additional growth of secondary roots. In my opinion, root pruning is not necessary in evergreen trees smaller than eight feet tall. What is essential is a type of soil that holds together solidly so remaining roots are not disturbed. The secondary roots support life while the primary roots are healing from the effect of being severed. The correct soil type, care while being dug, and careful replanting are the main factors in successful planting.

The state of Pennsylvania boasts of many nurseries that sell seedlings. Most suggest autumn planting as well as spring. I prefer spring planting, the earlier the better, but after anticipated ground freezing is over. When soil freezes the moisture within converts to ice. The fact that water expands when converted to ice is instrumental in ground heaving, a twelve-inch crust of the earth becoming thirteen or fourteen inches. When warm weather returns the ice melts to allow the soil to settle back to its former density. Autumn planted seedlings, particularly small ones, are raised upward by the heaving and, as spring rains resettle the soil, are left higher than originally planted. Planting too early in spring can also bring about this condition. In New York State the ideal planting month is April. The time varies—earlier southward and later in the north.

Seedlings are grown from seed collected from cones. That seed, like most seed, has to pass through a dormant period to grow. It also has to have the correct type of soil and moisture. It is a tiny seed that is scattered in narrow widths, or beds, so that laborers can reach in from sides to thin and remove weeds. Sales booklets speak of transplanted evergreens and give the impression that each tree is individually dug and replanted. What actually happens is a machine with flat cutting blade is drawn under the beds to cut long roots off, simply raising the width of the bed upward a fraction of an inch and dropping it back into place. This is usually done in the second, third, and fourth years. Thus a seedling is a one-year-old seedling, or a two-year-old transplant, and so on. Transplants develop a more extensive root system and generally are bushier and more sturdy than seedlings. Personally I prefer a twelve-inch size in a three-year transplant. Since length of root is counted in the size of a transplant, a twelve-inch size stands about eight inches above the ground after being planted. It also has lower branches intact, which is important if the seedling is being planted for lawns. Seedlings taller than twelve inches sometimes lose lower branching due to being crowded. In planting for cut Christmas trees, lower branching is relatively unimportant as they are usually cut from the tree to expose the lower trunk.

Seedlings, and that term describes transplants as well, are purchased in quantities of 500 or 1,000. Because the price of seedlings has risen in recent years nurseries will honor requests for as small an order as 100. They are placed in heavy waterproof paper with roots overlapping, tied securely in a bundle, and shipped directly to you. Parcel post, as well as private carriers, will deliver bundles containing as many as 1,000. Shipping instructions say to "heel in" upon being opened at arrival. "Heeling in" means setting the bundles upright in a dug trench and refilling it so all roots are below ground.

The area to be planted can be unworked or cultivated. If unworked it should be relatively free of quackgrass which, if dense, can choke newly planted seedlings. Ordinary weed and grass are no great problem. Poison ivy, if present, should be destroyed prior to planting. I use a long-handled, good grade shovel. I sharpen the round cutting edge with a flat mill file. In the field I stretch a line tightly to maintain a straight row. Knots in the line, or a couple turns of sticky tape, mark the spacing for each tree. I keep the line about forty-eight inches above ground so as to work under it without disturbing it. The bundle of plants is removed from, heel in, and shears are used to snip long roots and side dangling ones. The seedlings are separated one by one and placed in a pail with several inches of water. In the field the shovel blade is pushed into the ground in a vertical position, pressure against the handle opens a gap, the seedling is placed so the root is straight downward, and the blade withdrawn, using care not to disturb the root. A foot placed next to the seedling closes the gap to seal it. One person using this method can plant 100 seedlings per hour. In the 50-60,000 I have planted in past years I have come to expect about 98 percent of trees planted in this way to grow. On windy or bright sunny days, be certain the roots do not dry out while being carried in hand. On wet rainy days exposure is not a problem.

If the plan is to grow straight-trunked trees, additional care must be given each spring, or until trees become sturdy enough to stand alone. Each winter the weight of snow and ice, in addition to tall weeds and grasses, may cause seedlings to flatten. Unable to straighten without the help from human hands the tips will grow upward causing a crook in the trunk that is permanent. A crooked trunk in a seedling means a crooked trunk in the tree. When danger of heavy snow is past, walk the rows of seedlings and straighten those that need it by flexing them upward. Once they become self supporting this chore can cease.

Fertilize seedlings that require it, those planted in poor grade soil, by ringing each tree with about one tablespoon of a basic 10-10-10 fertilizer. If the analysis is 20-20-20, use half that amount. Keep the circle three inches distant from the stem to avoid burning. Do not get fertilizer on foliage as it will do damage. A second application can follow the first. If the first is applied in April the second can be applied in mid-June. Do not fertilize later than June.

A thirty-year-old Blue Spruce, which was transplanted from my nursery, in my yard.

A scattering of Blue Spruce trees growing in my nursery.

An expended gall, more noticeable because insects have gone.

A Colorado Blue Spruce with undeveloped leader due to injury by insect.

Same tree with one horizontal branch gently bent upright and tied to another branch for support.

Colorado Blue Spruce

Colorado Blue Spruce is one of the most important varieties of spruce trees. It grows in the wild in mid-western states, particularly the state of Colorado. The name derives from the state of Colorado and the tendency of branching to be multiple shades of blue. The name is misleading because all Colorados are not blue. On the average, in a given quantity of seedlings, about fifty percent will be more green than blue, forty percent will be mild to bright blue; only about ten percent will be the silvery blue that most people admire. The blue color is a powder produced on the exterior of needles in certain trees. This powder is more noticeable in small trees than in large ones because a greater proportion is new growth and the powder is produced only on new growth. The blue is enhanced by quality of soil, source of seedlings, and weather. When trees become dormant in September the production of powder ceases and that on the tree slowly begins to fade, washed off by rain, wind, and snow as winter commences. By spring only traces of it remains, usually on that part of the tree protected by drifting snow or on that side of the tree opposite prevailing winds. A tree, dug and placed in a storage area, will retain the full intensity of its coloring throughout the entire winter season. Naturally, more green trees do not have amounts of the blue powder to undergo noticeable change from one season to the next.

As stated, the amount of powder on blue trees is greater if trees are healthy and growing well. Replanted trees lose the ability to produce powder until such time as root systems become re-established. In contrasting the color of Colorados, do not confuse them with the Koster Blue. This patented tree, which originated in Germany, retains its blue sheen during the winter season. Koster Blue is a budded development not grown from seed, and the added work and time for growing to size makes it more costly. Koster Blue tends to be irregular as a young tree but will eventually straighten to be similar in shape to the Colorado.

If you examine the needles of Colorado Blue closely you will see that they are triangular in shape and sharply pointed. When cold they become stiff and can be irritating to unprotected skin. The mild rash usually lasts only a short time. Colorado needles grow completely around branches and are about one inch in length. This rugged tree is ideal for windswept locations, as the trees do not windburn on the exposed side. Growth in small trees is slow, normally from four to eight inches per season, but trees well established with extensive root systems may grow twelve to fourteen inches. A small tree that grows too rapidly should be pruned. Pruning consists of cutting part of the leader and a portion of side tips. My rule of thumb is to prune a tree that grows more than eight inches seasonally. That rule applies only to trees that can be pruned without the use of a ladder, and it is normally done in mid-June. The branches of Colorado Spruce grow directly upward at the top and horizontally at the sides. Pruning side branching is the cutting off of tips so the tree will grow more dense but less wide. Pruning the top is more difficult if the desire is to grow straight, upright trees. Look at the leader closely. You will see a center bud that will become next season's leader. The ring of buds surrounding the center bud will grow horizontally. Other buds, either as singles or clusters along the stem of the leader, also will grow outward rather than upward. Cutting the leader destroys the one that is destined to grow upward. There are ways to compensate. If you examine the growth of the leader at precise intervals you will note, by the thick clustering of needles separating from each other, that growth starts at the base. The process continues upward along the stem with the final inch added as the tip itself finishes the separation. Upward growth is now complete. Development will be needle length then bud growth in preparation for next year's branching.

If you examine the leader when growth reaches six inches and you notice the separation of needles complete to the half-way point you will know the leader will grow another six inches. If you cut two inches off the top, you are lessening growth by four inches and restricting it to a total of eight. But you have destroyed the upward bud. There are three ways to restructure. One is to do nothing. Nature will turn one or more of the horizontal growths upward in a gentle curve to become the new leader. The curve becomes a crook in the trunk that eventually is screened by additional branching. A second method is to permit side growths to gain length to about five inches, then gently bend the topmost growths upward so they support one another, and tie them together loosely with twine. In about two to three months the several will stiffen, the twine can be removed, the one most central left as is to become the new leader while all others are cut at the half-way point or close to the base. The purpose is always to maintain a single leader. The third method is to free the upper three inches of the stem of all new growths, then tie one growth below the three inch point to the stem using its strength as the support. Again, in time, that twine must be removed.

The horizontal branches of the Colorado extend outward from the trunk at a ninety-degree angle. It is the only one of the spruces to do this. As the tree ages the branches tend to slant downward from weight of the wood and foliage. Some encourage low branches to rest on the ground while continued growth causes the tips to curve upward. This saucer effect is only one of the several interesting shapings of the Colorado Blue Spruce.

As you begin to learn about trees, do not be disenchanted by the knowledge that almost all are subject to injury either by insect or fungi. The one advantage in control of insects is that they are predictable in habit and lifecycle, and they infest a particular tree. The Colorado has two major insects and several minor ones. The most common major one is Cooley's gall. This insect will not kill a tree, but the sight of expended galls hanging on the tips of branching after insects emerge is most annoying. The galls, which house several hundred insects each, become more visible as they dry and turn brown. Removing them now becomes a cosmetic operation. If the galls are in the green stage, and destroyed by burning or otherwise, the insects are also destroyed. Removal by hand can only be done on relatively small trees. This flying insect lays eggs at the base of buds in late autumn. The eggs are protected by a coating of woolly wax. The young hatch in about ten days to bore to the inside of the husk covering the undeveloped bud. In the spring the bud responds by enlarging to form the so-called gall.

While complete control is difficult, the best result comes by spraying with dormant oil in early spring. Dormant oil is a special oil that will mix with water to form a milky-like mixture. It destroys by forming an air-tight seal over insects, thus smothering them. It is available at garden stores and is not toxic; a simple washing of hands after use is the only precaution needed. Follow directions for quantities to be mixed. Apply the oil on a day with a temperature in the range of forty to eighty degrees, and thoroughly wet all branching above and below. A pesticide can be mixed with the mixture if desired. Apply dormant oil only one time per season.

The more serious insect to Colorado is the red spider. Mites, as they are often called, are spider-like in appearance; very tiny, they can be red, green, or dark in coloring. One indication of the presence of mites is the changing of the interior of a tree from green to rusty brown. Place a white sheet of paper under a suspected branch on a warm sunny day and jar the branch with a sharp blow from the fist. Mites are about the size of a sharp pencil dot, and the number that fall onto the paper tells if the infestation is mild or severe. There may be as many as several hundred. Do not pay attention to larger spiders, which are beneficial. Mites are sucking insects that multiply rapidly in hot dry weather. They can change the interior of a blue spruce from green to brown in a matter of weeks. Mites cannot fly and must be carried from tree to tree by other means, primarily wind, but also on the feet of birds and climbing animals. Infested trees in your neighborhood can cause yours to be infested also, but many trees complete an entire lifecycle without becoming infested. They say a poor man's way to rid a tree of mites is the thorough washing of branches with a pressurized stream of water. So pick up your water hose and wash your trees occasionally. It does work.

More effective, of course, is spraying the tree or trees with pesticide, then waiting for about a ten-day interval before spraying for a second time. Two good sprayings will destroy both living insects and those hatching from previously laid eggs. Your trees should remain free of insects for several years after this double spraying.

Other insects of the Blue Spruce are sawflies, needle miners, and bud worms. The first are green worms that feed on newly-formed needles to cause a ragged appearance. Unless sawfly young are numerous they do no lasting damage. Control is by pesticide. Needle miners, *Taniva albolineana* by name, are small worms that bore into the base of needles to cause them to turn brown and die. Indication is clusters of dead needles and webbing along the branches. Again, elimination is by thorough wetting with a pesticide. A similar cluster of webbing and needles in the inside of small crotching branches is an indication of bud worms. Probing the cluster will disclose a small, very active bright green worm about one-half inch long. Spraying the entire tree is effective, but if infestation is light I dab at the nests with a small paintbrush dipped in pesticide. This is not a common insect.

Blue spruce grow to sixty or seventy feet tall with a spread of about eighteen feet. Lawn trees are well rooted and seldom, if ever, blow over in strong wind. The wood has a strong, pungent odor. When used inside a house as a cut Christmas tree needle retention is excellent; however, the sharp pointed needles make hanging ornaments difficult. Rooted and balled trees make ideal living Christmas trees. More about those in a later chapter!

A White Spruce in my nursery.

A White Spruce heavily infested with red spider. Evidence is the browning of the lower interior of the tree extending upward through the middle.

White versus Black Hills Spruce

There may be differences between the White and Black Hills of which I am unaware. To my knowledge the main difference is in the color of the needles. White Spruce is gray to light gray in coloring with little or no deviation; Black Hills is a darker shade with variations of a bluish sheen in some trees. The appearance, rate of growth, type of soil to be planted in, as well as density of branching and angle upward of branches from the main trunk are all similar. Both can be planted closely to the other without noticeable differences.

The branches of both trees extend upward at about a forty-five degree angle to the trunk. The result is a tree more narrow than either the Blue or Norway and, at the same time, more dense. Even without pruning the trees achieve a density that prevents seeing through the tree; they are thus ideal for screening purposes. If growth is too vigorous the leader can be severed without special effort to develop a new one. Both tend to have cones on earlier than the Blue and Norway, the Blue not producing cones until the height of about twenty feet, the Norway about the same height, while the White and Black Hills cone at approximately eight feet. Both will grow in moderately moist soil. If uncertain about definition of moist soil, most people are aware that surface water can remain on the surface after a heavy rain. If the water remains for more than a twenty-four hour period the soil is too moist for evergreens. One method of determining moisture content is to dig a hole, fill it with water, and time its seepage into the soil. If water is present after twenty-four hours the soil is moist. That location is questionable for evergreens but if the site is raised above ground level by adding soil to create a mound evergreens may still be planted.

Galls on the White and Black Hills Spruces differ from those on the Norway only that they stand out as being red colored at first stage. After several days they revert to the normal green of the Norway. The galls are attached to the inner part of the branches and thus are not as noticeable as those on the Blue. Control is similar. Other insects may, from time to time, pose a problem to White and Black Hills, but in my years of experience gall is the major insect to watch for and control.

Norway Spruce tree about fifteen years old.

Row of mature Norway Spruce.

Norway Spruce

Norway is a fast-growing evergreen that will grow well in a much more moist planting site than will Blue Spruce. Its annual rate of growth varies from tree to tree, but can be as great as forty-eight inches. Normally the rate of growth is spoken of as being twenty-four inches compared to the Blue Spruce's twelve. It is an established fact that fast-growing trees have a shorter life span than do the slower-growing ones. Both the Blue and the Norway can be expected to continue growing and be healthy looking for a number of years, perhaps nearing or greater than the half-century mark. I assume the Blue lives slightly longer than does the Norway. In comparing rates of growth it is well to remember that, normally, the older the tree the greater the rate of growth. That holds true only up to the time when the particular specie attains maturity, that is a time for leveling off growth, and in still further time decline commences.

Norway has a uniform dark green color with no variation throughout the growing season. It is a vigorous tree and will send out multiple end tips that, because they are both heavy in weight and flexible, hang downward on small trees similar to fur on a shaggy-haired dog. Shearing (or pruning, which is another word to describe the same process) can be difficult at this time. It requires sliding the blade of the shears under a portion of the growth, lifting the shears upward and outward to estimate the length needed to be sheared, and cutting at that length. In time all growth, both that sheared close or that unsheared, will attain strength to support itself in its normal outward position. Cutting the leader, or leaders if there is more than one, is simple because the tree develops a new leader without outside assistance. Simply cut the top at the desired length. One of the pleasant characteristics of all spruce trees is that they can be neglected for a time and then by annual pruning brought back to the beautiful state they might have been otherwise. Some homeowners like the natural look. It means letting the tree, or trees, grow without human direction. All spruce can be grown in this manner. It simply means, don't prune at all.

Norway is subject to spruce gall aphids also, but the two insects that infest the Blue and Norway are different. Galls on a Norway can number into the thousands while those on the Blue generally are in the hundreds or less. Galls on Norway are not as large as those on Blue Spruce and are attached more solidly and more inwardly. They, however, are more prominent when forming, and removal by hand is easier. If some of the live branching is broken off in tearing loose the galls it is not a lasting damage. The gall in Norway is caused by the eastern gall aphid.

Norway can be attacked by red spider but is not as likely to become infested as is the Blue. If detected, control is similar.

Sawflies, needle miners, and bud worms, also can create problems to growers of Norway Spruce. Reread the control for Blue Spruce and repeat for Norway.

If trees, including other varieties of evergreens, show yellowing without apparent reason it can be due to depleted nutrients in the soil, or being in too wet a location. A tree doing well for several years can reverse itself if weather conditions change from a series of dry years to wet years. If soil depletion is suspected a sample of soil can be sent to the county USDA extension service, and tested to determine what is needed.

Norway grows to about the same height and diameter as does the Blue. Mature Norway gives the impression of branching laden with fur as the weight of foliage hangs downward from limbs. It, too, is a sturdy tree, withstanding the force of wind in summer and the weight of ice and snow in winter. Norway requires sunlight. If trees are planted closely together, lower limbs shed foliage and die. Used as a cut Christmas tree the needles drop freely after a few days in a warm house. As a living tree with roots and burlapped the likelihood of it dying are lessened, but survival depends on it being in a warm house only a short time.

My last remaining Englemann Spruce. Note the upright stance.

Closer view of Englemann branching.

Englemann Spruce

I became aware that there are those who visit nurseries to search for unusual plants when two well-dressed men visited one day. They stated their reason for coming and I agreed to show them an unnatural tree growing in the midst of my Blue Spruce. It was, at the time, about seven feet in height. I had declined to sell it previously because it was different. It had a blue sheen, similar to Blue Spruce, but its branching grew upward at an angle to the trunk. The needles were not as stiff, not as sharply pointed, and were longer and thicker. My expectation was deflated when I was informed it was simply a different variety, an Englemann Spruce rather than a Colorado Blue, but my interest remained high and the following spring I planted several hundred Englemann.

Those several hundred trees grew to size for selling and now grace the lawns of customers. I still admire this variety of tree. The upward sweep of branches gives it a natural density and a symmetrical shape that appears to need no pruning. The root system is a spreading one like the Blue, with digging actually easier because branches tie upward with less effort than the extended branches of the Blue. It does not have the bright silver-blue coloring of my bluest Blue Spruce but it does have interesting shades of blue.

A small percentage of my Englemann became infested with gall. Just as gall differs among the White, Norway, and Blue, the gall in the Englemann appears different also. It is larger than on the White, smaller than on the Blue, and adheres more tenaciously to the branching. I assume it can be controlled by application of a dormant oil in early spring or by one or more sprays with the proper amount of pesticide. Another educated guess is that this tree grows in the same well-drained soil as does the Blue, growing to fifty or sixty feet tall with a branch spread of fifteen feet. The name probably reflects the name of the man who first discovered it.

In foreground, a Balsam Fir about twelve years in age.

Close-up view of branching of Balsam Fir.

Balsam Fir

If the three firs, Balsam, Concolor, and Douglas, were entered into a beauty contest and I was the judge I would rate the Balsam first, Concolor second, and Douglas third. Perhaps I am prejudiced. When I first started to plant Balsam seedlings I didn't know they grow best in moist soil, and planted them along the ridge of high land. As I have stated before, moist land trees will grow in dry land but dry land trees will not grow in moist land. These proved not to be the exception. They grew quite well. One spring morning about 10A.M. I strolled to the ridge to check my Balsams. The sun shone brightly in a clear sky. The wind blew freely, sending gusts this way and that way, as is common in spring time. The trees were still wet with the previous night's dew. Balsams are trees of two colors, silvery white beneath the branching, dark green above. The breeze kept sweeping through the trees, uplifting the branching to create a dazzling effect as sunlight flashed through the clinging water droplets. They glistened like decorated indoor Christmas trees. They won my heart. That's why I give them first place.

Balsam is the only evergreen I know of that grows well in moist soils. It is a shallow-rooted tree that digs well and transplants well. The branches grow outward from the trunk in much the same fashion as the Blue Spruce. Consequently, the cutting of the leader is a delicate chore. I suggest using the same procedure as with the Blue, cutting the top at the desired length, then tying the uppermost growth in an upright position when they reach the length of three to five inches. Tie loosely so as to not prohibit further growth. When the group becomes rigid enough to be self-supporting, cut off all but the most central one. That one will become the leader.

Balsam will grow fifty to sixty feet tall with a spread of about eighteen feet. I know of no attacking insects but there may be some. If so, spray with a pesticide. This tree, like the Douglas, makes an ideal inside Christmas tree as its needle retention is good and its aroma pleasant.

A Concolor Fir with Blue Spruce in the background.
Tree is approximately seven years old.

Close-up view of Concolor.

Concolor Fir

The first Concolor Fir that I saw was one standing in a lawn in Pultneyville, New York. I was delivering another type of tree to the owner. I asked if I might examine it at close range. It was a tree I estimated at about thirty feet tall. The lower branches had been pruned to a five-foot height, so visibility from the house to the road remained unobscured. The tips of bottom branching formed a perfect circle, while others tapered upward to form a cone with the small end upward and nary a break in the side. I am assuming the branching would have remained close to the ground level had it been allowed to do so. The coloring was a milky green, if there is such a shade. The wood was smooth to the touch and gave the impression it was transparent, which, of course, it wasn't. The needles were heavy bodied, soft looking, and curled upward from entirely around the branches. Small brushes lathered with soap, I concluded, while looking at them.

Like the Englemann Spruce that I first had to identify before purchasing seedlings, I now ordered several hundred Concolors. I planted them in what I considered good grade soil that was neither too wet nor too dry. It seems to me they took forever to grow but finally they did and now, twenty years later, all but three have been dug and sold. I had no problem with insects, did no pruning, did no spraying. The color varied with shades of milky-green to bluish-green. The root is a spreading one comparable to spruces, and digging for transplanting was comparably easy. The success of transplanted trees, if I remember correctly, was 100 percent. Most were dug in the height range of five to six feet and while growth was only inches per year in the seedling size it increased to about eight to ten inches in larger trees. Those that plant seedlings, regardless of type, will learn that all do not grow at the same rate. Some will inch upward, others will grow as if anxious to be large as soon as possible. If you plant trees closely with the thought of removing the larger ones first, you will find several in close proximity that grow at the same fast rate. That is Murphy's law, so I am told.

Douglas Fir in my nursery.

Closer view of Douglas foliage.

Douglas Fir

Douglas Fir has become a very popular cut Christmas tree in recent years. The reason for this is congested homes where space for the placing of a one-time item such as a Christmas tree is limited. Also, modern-type shag rugs don't surrender dropped needles from trees easily. The Douglas, with its good needle retention plus rather narrow shape, appeals to many homeowners. In addition the odor of a Douglas is pleasant. All firs have differing odors when a branch is broken, and all are pleasing ones. That odor is slowly released into the air as the trees dry in the warmer air of the inside. Pines also have fragrant odors, as do most of the spruces. The one exception might be the Blue which has a strong odor, varying from tree to tree; occasionally one may even be offensive. Fortunately Blue Spruce is a dense wooded tree and odor release is scant. If one is unhappy with the natural odor one can always spray the tree with another scent of his or her choice.

As a landscaping plant the Douglas is attractive. The range of coloring in foliage is from light green to light blue. The color, as in the Blue Spruce, is the result of heredity with soil, weather, and health contributors. If soil was the important factor then all trees in a given area would be the same shade of color. If weather was the main factor the color would vary from year to year. It does not. So heredity must be the compelling force, with others more important in maintaining health.

Douglas needs to be pruned if the desire is strong, good-looking trees. The branches sweep upward from the trunk which makes maintenance of a leader relatively simple. Pruning is usually done in mid-June and clipping off of excess growth is greatest near the top of the tree and less as one moves down the sides. Pruning of evergreens can be done at any time of year, as with almost all other trees and bushes. The two exceptions are Sugar Maple and Grape, which should not be pruned to any degree when sap is flowing. I will state that neither should be pruned in the months of March and April.

Douglas is a spreading root tree and digs easily. It is not subject to either gall or scale. There is, however, a two-year cycle of the Blue Spruce gall that alternates between the two. Indication are tiny cottony balls adhering to foliage. Close examination will reveal an insect within the cotton. If trees are sprayed with a pesticide, the insects will die. The cotton remains to be removed in time by natural elements such as rainfall and wind. Implied by this knowledge is a mild warning not to plant Blue Spruce and Douglas Fir too closely together. If the gall in Blue Spruce is under control the infestation of Douglas will not occur. If the cycle of gall in the Douglas is treated effectively then the likelihood of gall in Blue Spruce is lessened. There is also the possibility that both varieties will grow strong and beautiful without ever becoming part of the lifecycle of the gall.

A row of upright American Arborvitie beginning to close rank at close to ground level. These plants are about eight years old.

A hedge of mature Arborvitie that has been topped at an eight-foot size.

Arborvitie

I have described spruces with triangular needles, pines with round, firs with flat. Now there are two still more, Arborvitie with lacey-type flat leaves and Junipers with feathery leaves. Let us deal with Arborvitie first. Like other varieties of evergreens Arborvitie comes in many shapes and sizes. A common one, *Thuja Occidentalis*, which is the Latin name, is native to North America and grows as tall as sixty feet. Most of the varieties used in landscaping are low growing ones. The American upright grows to twenty or thirty feet, so I am informed, if it is not topped as is often the case. It is a narrow tree with the diameter of branching between four and five feet and is usually planted at four-foot centers so as to leave no openings between trees at maturity. Arborvitie has a flat leaf, or what appears to be a flat leaf, but actually is a series of leaves from a common stem on the same plane. Examine one closely. It looks like tightly braided human hair. In the average year about fifty percent of trees bear seeds. Like the leaves, the seeds are strung together in short strings. They are green during the summer, ripening to brown as winter comes in. Wind, rain, and snow during cold weather break them from the mother tree to scatter in attempt to find fertile soil to start a new life. Arborvitie is used in many ways—along property lines, to furnish privacy to lawns and swimming pools, to enhance housing by being planted at door entrances or at the far corners. The American remains green all summer long, but like pines, changes to a brownish tinge at approach of winter. It also sheds all year-old leaves in late autumn, causing worry to the uninformed. In a short span of time the foliage drop ends until the conclusion of another year. Other types are:

Prymidial, a cone-shaped type growing to four feet formed by several stems;

Hetzi and Nigra, two that are low growing and retain green summer coloring;

Global, a low type that forms a ball-like top; and

Golden, another low variety that carries the brown tips of winter throughout the summer as well.

Arborvitie has a spreading root system, it digs and transplants well; it grows best in well drained soils but will tolerate moisture. Insects and diseases appear to be minor problems. I have grown several thousand without the need to spray. Also without the need to prune. Some grow in clumps of two or three. Tall clumps need tying together in winter to prevent breakage from the weight of ice and snow.

Blue Spruce selected by a customer.

Branches tied upward in preparation for digging.

Same tree dug and burlapped. Plank assisted in raising it out of hole to ground level.

Tree planted in customer's yard. Tie rope has been removed. Burlap is under ground.

How To Dig and Burlap an Evergreen Tree

Digging any tree is a task made easier by experience. My purpose in writing this is to allow you to use my experience to your advantage, providing you read and follow it. The first thing to know is that hidden below ground is the root structure.

All spruces have a spreading root system, one that normally extends out in several directions from the trunk. In moist soils roots tend to remain closer to the surface, in dry soils to extend more deeply. Even in the dry soils a six-foot-tall tree can be expected not to root deeper than eighteen to twenty-four inches. In moist soils about twelve inches is most common. The roots may extend outward to distances approaching six to eight feet. Trees in moist soil extend out more than those in dry soil. Dry soils are gravel, sand, or normal soils on ridges or hilltops. Moist soils are clay mixtures, soil of any description bordering on marsh land, any soil lacking drainage. Spruces are dry-soil trees and will grow better and more attractively if planted in the proper soil. If the site is inclined to be wet and yet the desire for spruce is strong, a mound of three to four inches higher than the surrounding ground can be constructed for each planting. If the tree, or trees, can be established each will adapt to the soil conditions to become reasonably good-looking trees.

In digging trees, roots must be cut. Larger trees necessarily have more root cut in the digging than do smaller ones. The normal diameter of ball is about twenty-four inches for trees under three feet tall, and up to thirty-six inches for those six feet tall. It is better to have a smaller, solid, compact ball than a larger, loosely textured one.

The tools needed are: a long-handled pointed shovel with the edge sharpened with a flat mill file; a burlap square about forty-eight inches wide for the larger sized tree; about fifteen common eight nails, a small quarter-inch-diameter rope about twenty feet in length. The purpose for the rope is to tie branches upward to protect the end tips and also make the digging easier. Select a point near to the top of the tree where the diameter of the stem will give strong support and tie one end of the rope to it. Reach down to some bottom branches and lift them upward, slip the rope underneath so that a second turn around the trunk will hold them in the uplifted position. Continue doing this until all interfering branches are out of the way. Next, place the point of the shovel up against the trunk at ground level and use the heel of the shovel as the circumference of the circle to be dug. Push the shovel into the soil to full depth of the blade on this circumference with a slight tilt to the inward. Roots encountered can be cut with the blade of the shovel, or with a hand saw, or clippers. Cut ends cleanly without splintering. Once the first circle is complete, cut a second one four to five inches larger in radius than the first one and remove all soil between the two. Continue to dig downward and inward until all holding roots are severed and the tree, with its attached ball of earth, will tilt freely in the hole. Tilt it one way and place the burlap beneath the ball in such a manner that in tilting it the opposite way the burlap can be unrolled, or tugged on, until the ball sits in the exact center.

The main purpose in burlapping a ball of earth is to hold it intact so that roots remain undisturbed. Make an effort to tighten the burlap securely with that purpose in mind. The first step is to pull opposing ends of the square across each other, and press a nail through both layers to sustain the pull you made. Once the opposite pairs are secure the loose folds still remaining can be pulled taut across the pairs and pinned also. The pinning nail should always be crossways to pull on the burlap.

Your tree is now ready to be lifted from the hole. It can be done physically, or slid up a plank to ground level. The same plank can assist in raising the tree to the platform of a truck.

Planting an Evergreen Tree

The directions previously given for planting a balled tree are similar to those being given now for planting an evergreen, except this will give more detail. If the planting is being done by the same person or persons who dug it, the branches can remain in the tied position for ease in replanting it. If a marking, in the form of a cloth strip or piece of twine, is tied on the most favorable side of the tree then the tree can be positioned in its new hole to best advantage. Evergreens tend to be heavier branched on the south side of the tree due to additional sunlight. If the replanting is to be done by someone other than the person who dug it, the judgment of which side faces which direction can be made prior to its replanting. Let's assume all is ready for replanting.

Mark the center of the location with a stake in the ground or a stone placed on top. Measure the diameter of the ball on the tree to be planted. Cut a circle around the marking about four inches larger than that measured diameter. Undercut sod, if present, and lay it aside. Cut the sides of the hole straight downward to a depth of about three inches deeper than the depth of the ball, and excavate soil so that the bottom of the hole is even. Next, return to the hole a portion of the removed soil. Add a five-gallon pail of moderately packed peat and sufficient clean water so that when all three are mixed the result is a thick, and still fluid, mixture. In spring planting a cup full of a basic 10-10-10 fertilizer can also be added and mixed with the other ingredients. (In autumn plantings the fertilizer application should be delayed until the following spring and applied to the ground surface beneath the drip edges of the tree.) Leaving the burlap on the ball with nails intact, or ties intact, slide the ball into the mixture and walk around the circumference, slowly pressing it down until the top of the ball is level with the surrounding ground. Allow time for moisture to be absorbed before adding more soil, then pack it firmly by foot and body weight so no cavities remain. If the tree is to be staked maintain ground level with top of ball. If the tree is small enough so as to not require staking, three or four inches of soil can be heaped on top of ball to hold it more securely.

Frequency of spring rains determines the need for watering. Normally, a hand-held hose with a moderate spray will water sufficiently in about a two-minute time period. Do this twice a month, particularly in the dryer months of July through September, the first year. Do not overwater. Do not allow running water to wet the tree and ground for long periods of time.

Please note: If the hole is being dug by machine, or made wider and deeper for any reason, be certain the fill is watered and firmly packed before planting the tree. Earth settling beneath the ball is not conducive to redevelopment of new roots. Do not line the bottom of the hole with stone, thinking (erroneously) that rocks will conserve moisture. If plantings are in sand or gravel the top of ball can be set one to two inches below ground level. If in doubt as to type of soil keep the ball level with the ground.

Staking is making the evergreen more secure. Needed are three stakes about eighteen inches in length and two inches in diameter. Drill a small hole near the top of each stake. Drive them into the soil about three inches outside the dug hole, slanting the stakes outward and equidistant from each other. Needed also are three short pieces of rubber hose and wire in a twelve or fourteen gauge. Thread one end of a wire through the hose and wrap it around the stem of the tree approximately eighteen inches from the top. Twist the wire so that it is secure but still loose around the stem. Carry the opposite end of wire to the stake, thread through the stake hole and pull tight to secure. Individual stakes can now be driven slightly deeper to straighten the tree. Make all the wires tight but not so tight as to be taut. For trees six feet tall and under, stakes should remain one season, for larger trees two seasons.

Please note also: If the wrapping burlap is not common burlap (usually uncommon burlap is dyed bright green), remove it entirely before planting. If strong cord is used to tie the burlap to the ball cut any that ties around the base of the trunk, but only after the tree is fully planted.

Pines

Pines are the darlings of real estate developers because they grow so rapidly. There are many varieties of pines. However I will limit description to only those that are most useful in landscaping. The differences between spruce and pine are so obvious that it is difficult to understand why so many customers confuse the two. Pines have round needles. In the three I plan to describe the length of needle varies from one to five inches, Scotch having the shortest, White the medium length, and Austrian the longest. Pine needles grow in clusters of two, three, and five. Pines discard all year-old needles seasonally and new needles turn a dull brown as cold weather comes. This yellowing commences on the tips of needles on the south, or sunlight, side and continues quite rapidly to the northern side as well. As the yellowing moves from the tip downward on the needle the entire tree takes on a yellow cast. About the same time this happens the shedding of old needles takes place. By Christmas time the yellowing is complete and most old needles have fallen.

Pines have tap roots with only minor secondary growth. Consequently, for successful planting, most pines need to be root pruned for several years prior to being transplanted. This is particularly important if trees are more than forty-eight inches in height. Because the root grows deeply and narrowly small trees can be dug and transplanted if care is taken to dig deeply and keep the ball of earth intact.

Additional varieties of pines are as follows:

Red Canadian; a tree growing primarily in Canada. It grows as tall as eighty feet and is valued for its timber.

Yellow; an eastern United States tree also valued for wood.

Jersey; a southern United States tree valuable for tar, pitch, turpentine, resin, and timber.

Pitch; similar to above and valued for same products.

Sabine's; a California pine with soft needles as long as fourteen inches. This tree can reach 120 feet in height if soil conditions are favorable.

Stone Pine; a European tree growing to sixty feet with a trunk free of branches.

Pinaster; often called cluster pine, it is common throughout Europe and Asia. It is often planted in barren sandy areas to help prevent the sand from drifting in strong wind.

Their fast growth—one can expect three to four feet per season after trees become well established—make pines ideal as background trees with spruce planted in the fore. Builders of apartments and condominiums use pines because they are showy, and they grow wide as well as fast. Also pines grow well in soil surrounding multiple buildings, which is not nurtured as carefully as that around private homes. Please read on for a more complete description of the three most common pines.

Unpruned Scotch Pine growing in the wild.

Properly cared-for Scotch Pine.

Scotch Pine

A consensus of opinion from those who grow evergreens for landscaping and from the cut Christmas tree trade would likely be that, of the three most commonly used pines, the Scotch is the most valuable. Scotch grows rapidly and holds up well under adverse weather conditions, rarely if ever breaking from the weight of ice and snow. It grows well in soil considered poor grade by known standards, damage from insects is minor and almost always temporary, and the Scotch seems to appeal to both the mind and the heart.

All pines grown for cut Christmas trees require pruning from early age on. Most used in landscaping also are pruned although occasionally individuals may prefer the untrimmed, or natural, look. Pines do not grow secondary growth between the tiers of branching as do spruces. A pine neglected even for a single year cannot be corrected. Consequently the aim of growers is to shorten the distances between seasonal branching to achieve density. The length of needles also contributes to density. Most of the seed used in the United States comes from Europe, where the growing of pines is very common in all countries and nearby islands. The length of needle differs with the source of seed, with the shorter needle in the more southern countries. The strains are named after the country of source, hence the Italian, the Spanish, Turkish, Irish strain, and so on. The length of needles in the French and Spanish strains is approximately one inch. Needles on the Riga strain from Latvia on the Baltic Sea can be three to four inches long. The additional length gives greater density during the growing season but has imperfections for those that grow this variety as a cut Christmas tree. Let me explain. All pines have the characteristic of converting from summer green to winter yellowing when cold weather approaches. The longer needle yellows more quickly than the shorter. The yellowing begins at the tips of needles on the sunlight side of the tree and slowly spreads to the opposite side also. As the yellow tinge engulfs the entire tree, the tree takes on an unhealthy appearance. Cutting the tree prior to the start of the yellowing process stops the process. The question arises, how soon to cut? Trees cut too early dry out before they are offered for sale. Trees cut early do not drop last season's needles as readily as do standing trees. I concentrated on storing, piling trees atop one another and wetting branches frequently, which was fine except that bottom trees flattened from the weight of those on top. Then I decided to leave the trees as they were cut from the stump. The cooling weather, with its frequent rains and heavy dews, kept trees moist until time to place them on display. Bottoms had to be recut, lower branches severed for tree stands, and clinging old needles removed by hand. No wonder the price of cut Christmas trees is escalating. Now, for the growing itself.

Scotch Pine for landscaping needs scant care excepting alertness for insects. Most have been root pruned prior to being dug. Some owners like the natural look, the growing to mature trees without attempting to increase density. Others prefer a cultivated appearance. Either method can produce beautiful trees.

When pine seedlings are planted the first indications of growth are upward projections sometimes referred to as candle sticks. The growth upward is usually greater than growth to the side. Unlike with spruces, when candles are cut off to restrict growth the needles closest to the cut will develop buds at the base that will ultimately become branching. This bud development occurs only when the tip is cut while in the flexible, or elongating, stage. Like spruce growth, the length of pine growth can be reasonably estimated by comparing the separation of needles at the base of the candle as compared to those not yet separated. This is important in pruning and must be done while candles are growing. If an error is made, cutting too short or not cutting enough, the only result will be shorter or longer distances between that season's branching. Nature often varies growth in a similar manner. Once the cut is made and buds develop there may be several leaders instead of the necessary one. At a time later in the summer, or in the fall, return to each tree to cut away all but the most central one. They can be entirely removed, or partly removed. This is in development of a new leader. Cuttings to control width can be left as they are.

The insects that infest pines are scale, saw flies, and pine shoot moth. Scale is detected by unhealthy appearance with multiple, elongated, white (lime-like) attachments to the surface of needles. The insect is a sucking one that can destroy even a mature tree if not checked. For two weeks each June it breaks out of its secreted house to mate and lay eggs. In this crawling stage, when the insects can be seen with the aid of a magnifying glass, they are subject to control by a normal pesticide spray. If not curtailed at this time the young move to new needles to pierce the skin and, at the same time, secrete a fluid for enclosing each in a protective house. Pesticides no longer give control but dormant oil will. This oil mixes with water to form a seal over the shell houses to smother the insects.

As stated previously it has to be applied when temperatures are between forty and eighty degrees, when weather promises to remain dry for twenty-four hours, and applied only one time. Pesticides can be applied as often as desired, but keep in mind that both pesticides and dormant oils pollute both air and ground water.

Sawfly worms, a stage in sawfly development, are a yearly threat to pines. Hatching from a cluster of eggs, the green worms enlarge by feeding on needles. The worms have the unusual characteristic of moving in unison if disturbed. They confine their destruction to a single branch until the food supply diminishes, then they move to another branch. When the worms are tightly congested a single blast from a spray gun will end the damage but later movement makes it necessary to spray the entire tree. It is fortunate for control that the insects are so predictable; the worms all hatch at about the same date so control can be accomplished shortly after.

Pine shoot moth is a flying insect that, I am informed, lays a single egg at the base of a developing bud. The egg hatches to a dark-headed white worm that bores to the interior of the branch, eventually causing it to die. That branch stands out as being dead against the green background of the living ones. It should be clipped off at a point two to three inches into the living wood and destroyed by burning. Usually damage from this moth is not extensive.

Other insects, if detected, can be eliminated by pesticide spraying.

A mature White Pine in a neighboring yard.

Close-up of White Pine's long, soft needles.

White Pine

White Pines are beautiful tall trees that grow best in rich, well-drained soils while in the protection of other trees. Needles are approximately four inches in length, soft and flexible to the touch, and grow in clusters of five. White Pine is the only pine growing clusters of five needles, all others being in the twos and threes. In addition to protection from other close growing trees can be buildings, hills on the prevailing wind side, or other natural or unnatural terrain. White Pine can be an ideal lawn tree. It is also important as a lumber tree, the wood being light, soft, strong, and unusually straight-grained. Trees will grow upward to seventy feet and retain lower branches if not too close to other trees. Thus its beauty is an individual more than as a windbreak.

White Pine is subject to the same insects that attack other pines, and control is similar. In addition, White Pine is a possible host to blister bust, a fungus which destroys inner bark. Attacked by this fungus is not a common occurrence and its likelihood is diminished if there are no currant or gooseberry bushes in the vicinity. These two bushes are partners in the lifecycle of the fungus. The White Pine weevil also can destroy the leader, but a new leader can be reconstructed as with other pines. Pruning to add density is done as with other pines and done at the same time of year. And, as with other pines, discarded needles in autumn—along with larger cones—litter lawns with debris. Needles can be utilized as filling for pine-scented pillows and cones used to decorate Christmas wreaths.

Austrian Pine about seven years of age.

A closer view of the Austrian Pine.
Notice the prominent buds for next season's growth.

Austrian Pine

There are differences in pines that allow one to be suitable for a given purpose and another one not. The Austrian, with its four- to five-inch length needle, requires more cleaning up after needle drop in late autumn. Also the cleaning out of dead needles for use as a cut Christmas tree is more difficult. If one overcomes that minor obstacle one confronts the four- to five-inch diameter trunk of trees that have been pruned to enhance the foliage, allowing diameters of stems to increase beyond the normal. Such large stems can also be a problem with Scotch Pine. I solve it by centering a thirty-six by thirty-six inch square of three-quarter-inch plywood to the squared butt of the tree and nailing it securely with size 30 nails. This prevents watering the tree but since needle retention on pines is excellent the need for watering is not as important as with other varieties. It dos not solve the width problem as Austrians tend to be wide as well as stocky.

Austrians can be beautiful trees in landscaping. The cones on bearing trees enhance the beauty. Normally, trees that are healthy when planted can go a lifetime without insects. If scale is seen on one branch and that branch treated with oil, the need to spray the entire tree becomes unnecessary. Scale usually spreads by a single infection. Saw fly worms appear to attack trees in smaller sizes than in mature trees. Even an occasional dead twig caused by the pine shoot moth can be neglected without worry about increased infection the following season. Because pines grow wide, care must be given to planting distances between trees. Trees set too closely will grow with intertwining branching, but control of insects is made more difficult as insects have easy access from tree to tree. As with Scotch, the Austrian makes a good background tree with the greener spruce planted in the fore.

Junipers in foreground with Evergreens and other trees in background.

Taxus planted along a raised deck. Blue spruce trees in far rear.

Taxus, Yews, and Junipers

I do not grow any of the above in my nursery but they are so important to landscaping that I would be negligent in not attempting to describe them. Yews and Taxus are so similar as to be interchangeable. They are found in Europe as large evergreen trees. The dwarf varieties we use are developments by Japan and other countries. I will explain them briefly.

Japanese Capitata Cuspidata; a four- to five-foot size yew with a broad base.

Adams Columnar; a similar but narrower variety.

Brown's; a compact yew with dark green, waxy foliage. One of the best.

Hatfield; a slow growing variety resembling the Japanese Cuspidata.

Hick's; a more narrow yew with rich, glossy, bright green foliage.

Ward's; a smaller variety with a density common to slow growing plants.

These are the names and descriptions of the most popular yews used to beautify homes by screening the foundations. They can be used in other ways as well.

Junipers are used in many of the same ways as yews. Junipers differ from yews in that the foliage is feathery shape rather than the small rounded leaf shape. Junipers can be green, grey, blue, or silver. Following are names of a few.

Chinensis San Jose; a prostrate type growing wide but less than one foot high. It has rather coarse texture but is extremely hardy. It is a spreading juniper.

Blue Pfitzer; a spreading type that grows to three or four feet but can be kept much lower by yearly pruning. Its feathery leaf is fragile looking and quite blue; however it is a hardy strain and withstands winter's offerings with little effect.

Ames Juniper; a greyish-blue variety that grows to six or seven feet if not pruned.

Armstrongi; a blue-green with soft foliage growing to four feet.

Pfitzeriana Glauca; a blue-grey growing to three or four feet.

Hetzi and Pfizer; both spreading type junipers with grey-green coloring.

Spreading junipers require no particular care but uprights occasionally need to be wrapped in burlap and tied with cord to prevent the several stems from being separated by weight of ice or snow.

Insects in junipers and yews are confined to scale, and control is by wetting the foliage with a dormant oil mixture. One application per season, and only when scale are present, is all that needs to be done. Yews, Taxus, and Junipers are generally intermixed along house foundations at the pleasure of the owner.

Flowering Bushes

The terms "shrub" and "bush" describe low-growing hardwood plants with several stems. I will use the term bush to describe those I have grown and of which have personal knowledge. Most bushes require full sunlight. A few will do well in reflected sunlight. Few will grow in deep shade. Most bushes do best in well-drained soils. A scattering, such as Pussy Willow and Redosier Dogwood as example, require moist soils. The lifespan of bushes is comparable to that of trees. Bushes, being as small as they are, are usually purchased as bare rooted, meaning the roots are not encased in a dirt ball. The roots of bare rooted bushes are protected from drying by being wrapped in a moist material, usually peat, or moss, and the whole packaged in plastic sheet or bag. Do not let the roots dry to even a mild degree prior to planting. If the bushes are container grown, slide the ball out of the container and straighten any roots that might have grown to circle the inside of the container. Keep the interior of the ball as intact as possible. In planting either container grown or bare rooted plants, dig the hole sufficiently wide to accommodate the roots' full extension. Place two to three inches of soil mixed with peat in the bottom of the hole, set the root mass on top and hold the plant firmly as more soil-peat mixture is added. Roots need to be directed evenly and the planting mixture worked in and around so no cavities remain. When soil reaches to within inches of the top, fill the hole with clean water, let the soil settle, pack it firmly, then add more soil to fill the hole to ground level.

Bushes that are balled and burlapped need only to be planted in the same manner as in planting a tree. Look for tree planting directions elsewhere in this book.

The bushes I plan to describe are not necessarily in order of importance. Some varieties are rare but most can be ordered from retail nurseries. Bushes have universal names in Latin but have prevailing language names as well. Ask for each by name.

Fifty-year-old Mock Orange bush in blossom.

Closer view of Mock Orange.

Mock Orange

Mock Orange probably got its name from its similarity to the orange tree blossom. This interesting bush grows to an eight-foot height with a spread of about five feet. Its life span is longer than fifty years. The blossom varies in size with variety, the largest being nearly two inches in diameter. Petals are snow white surrounding a bright yellow center. Fragrance varies with type of bush but fragrant ones fill surrounding air with sweet scent when blossoming. Blossoms last almost two weeks. Mock Orange requires dry soil and full sunshine to be at its best. It can be pruned to be kept at a lower height or left unpruned. In either case it blossoms seasonally without fail. Insects appear to not be a problem, nor is mildew or fungi so there is no need to spray. The following will assist in selecting single or double flowering varieties. Ask for it by name.

Sweet Mock Orange: a standard, old-fashioned variety; very sweet odor, hardy, blossoms in mid-May, grows to about eight feet.

Silvia: a new introduction from Canada; fragrant double white blossoms, deeply serrated foliage, hardy, blossoms in May.

Snowstorm: a German development; is hardy, compact, grows to five feet, blossom resembles carnations, flowers in mid to late May.

Innocence: very fragrant single white blossom with thin branching, causing it to arch downward; height unknown.

Virginal Everblooming: a compact six-foot variety with continuous double white, waxy-looking blossoms.

Minnesota: another everblooming variety; flowers are small and include both single and double white blossoms.

Red Weigela being used as a foundation planting.

Pink Weigela in full shade at northwest corner of house.

Weigela

Weigela is a flowering bush that grows to a five-foot height and the same in diameter. The flowers come in late May, trumpet-shaped blossoms that are generally numerous to give the entire bush a mass of color. Foliage is attractive, with leaves either plain or variegated depending on variety. The blossom of the variegated is light pink. Weigela will grow well in full sunlight, and is one of the few flowering bushes that will grow in shade and continue to flower. Plants are usually bare rooted in an eighteen-inch to two-foot size. The planting site should be relatively dry. Weigela should be pruned yearly to maintain its shape, as it is a vigorous grower. It can be a hedge material planted at five-foot spacings. It also can be planted within twelve inches of foundations. The one yellow variety is not as vigorous a grower as the others. Ask for it by name:

Eva Rathke: one of the best; blossom is scarlet.

Bristol Ruby: vigorous, with very dark red flowers.

Venusta: an early blooming pink variety.

Java: a bright red.

Vaniceki: another bright red.

Lutea: an unusual yellow.

Henderson: a more upright variety with crimson buds developing into deep pink flowers.

Weigela's foliage turns crimson red in late Autumn prior to dropping. Normally it is free of insects and requires no particular care, except the minor pruning seasonally.

A group of P. G. Hydrangea bushes in full bloom in mid-August. These bushes have bloomed yearly for the past fifty years.

Close-up view of P. G. Hydrangea.

Hydrangea

If you have seen bushes in cemeteries and other locations, waving their large white panicle blossoms in the breeze, you have observed the Pee Gee Hydrangea. I am informed the origin of the name is unknown. The plant itself is a bulbous, thick-rooted plant that grows best in well drained soil. It is a vigorous grower, pushing out two to three feet of stem growth seasonally, with green clustered flowers at the tips. The leafing along the stems is green and attractive. As July edges into August the green clusters expand into large white panicles varying in size from six to twelve inches in length. Widths vary from six to nine inches. The odor is neither pleasant or unpleasant. Slowly, after several showy weeks the south, or sunlight side, of the panicles begins turning to pink. The converting to pink continues until frost stills the process. Then foliage dulls to drop from the stems, the panicles turn brown also but refuse to fall until winter's ice and snow break the stems. A precaution is to cut the stems close to the parent wood to prevent added height in mature plants. Most grow to about eight feet. Growing bushes need more length left of stems to add height. If blossoms are cut with long stems just prior to frosting they, along with foliage, can be placed in waterless vases for up to a full year. Bushes are relatively narrow so planting four in diamond fashion, or three in triangle position, gives a pleasant grouping. Distance in planting varies with three feet commonly used as center to center. Pee Gee's lifespan is more than fifty years.

Blue Hydrangea, called Nikko Blue, is a low growing hydrangea with various shades of blue blossoms. The blossoms are smaller and more rounded shaped than the Pee Gee. Also structure wood dies back to ground level each year to send up new growth in spring. The Blue, like the Pee Gee, needs rich well-drained soil. The strength of the blue in blossoms varies with the chemistry of the soil. Sometimes, additives are added to the soil in an attempt to enhance the blue coloring. The Blue is often planted against house foundations for beauty as well as protection from wind. Insects are not bothersome to either the Blue or the Pee Gee.

Rose bushes in blossom in late September on east side of building.

Roses

In describing roses I will have to rely on information written in books. I have not grown roses but feel they are so important to landscaping that I cannot neglect them. General knowledge is that the rose, like most other flowers, was taken from the wild and transformed into the countless varieties that are available from today's nurseries. The natural rose was, and is, a single petaled flower with intense fragrance that grows on prickly, brambled bushes. The character of the bush has changed, certainly the flower itself has changed, but the prickly wood support remains pretty much as it was.

Roses are the product of countries within the cooler northern hemisphere. Most require an adequate water supply but will not grow well in too moist a soil. Most require full sunshine but can get by with several hours of reflected sunshine, particularly that of later afternoon. Like the peach some are susceptible to winter injury due to ground freeze, so the rooted area should be mulched during winter with straw, leaves, or other materials. Plant new bushes in spring rather than autumn because of the danger of winter freeze. Most rose bushes are sold as bare rooted plants. Take care that the roots do not dry out prior to planting. The bulge at the base of the plant is the graft point. It should be about at ground level after planting. The hole for the normal short-stemmed rose is twelve inches in depth by eighteen inches in diameter. Follow directions as for planting other bare rooted stock. A good grade soil is important for growth.

Roses are subject to injury by insects, scale, and fungi, the latter in the form of mildew and black spot. Black spot is circular dark spots with irregular margins on leaf surface. When infestation is severe foliage becomes yellow and drops. It, like mildew, is more common in extended wet periods. Control is a preventative spraying with fungicide spray, or preventing spreading of the disease by fungicide spray after infestation. Scale is controlled by application of dormant oil as explained earlier. Feeding insects are controlled by pesticide sprays.

Rose bushes need occasional pruning. In early spring remove all dead wood, all weak upright shoots, and cut remaining shoots back to a twenty-four to thirty-inch length. Ramblers and climbing roses may need pruning to lessen density. Make clean cuts with a sharp-edged shearing tool.

The spacing of new bushes depends on variety. Teas are generally planted two to three feet apart. Floribundas and Polyanthas are from three to four feet. Upright bushes require about five-foot distances, while climbers need from eight to ten feet. Roses are classified by growing characteristics into descriptive names. They are named the following:

Hybrid Teas are everblooming roses which have relatively small flowers with long stems.

Floribundas are upright bushes with tea-sized roses growing in clusters.

Polyanthas are clustered roses, smaller than teas, but with clusters larger than floribundas.

Hybrid Perpetuals are variations of old-fashioned roses. They have generally large flowers with imperfections, but are hardy and require but little care.

Shrub Roses are wild species that are sometimes used in landscaping.

Tree Roses are a limited number that grow on strong upright wood.

Miniature are those growing not more than eighteen inches tall. They are used in rock gardens.

Ramblers are fast-growing cane types with small flowers.

Large-Flowered Climbers are ramblers with larger flowers.

Everblooming Climbers, Climbing Teas, Climbing Polyanthas, and Climbing Floribundas are several types that adapt to being trained to grow to heights by means of a trellis or other support.

The following are varieties, listed in order of importance some years ago by the American Rose Association. That evaluation remains accurate.

In the Red Hybrid Teas are: Crimson Glory, Charlotte Armstrong, Étoile de Hollande, Christopher Stone, Poinsettia, Red Radiance, and Red Dutchess.

Among the Yellow Teas are: Eclipse, Golden Dawn, and McGredy's Yellow.

Pink Hybrid Teas are: Dainty Bess, Picture, Curley Pink, Radiance, and Pink Satin.

White Hybrid Teas are: Pedralbes, McGredy's Ivory, Snowbird, and Mme. Jules Bouche.

Blend Roses are: Peace, Pres. Herbert Hoover, Sutter's Gold, Mission Bells, and California.

Among the Floribundas are: Red Pinocchio, Frensham, both red; Rosenelfe, Betty Prior, and Nearly Wild, pink varieties; Goldilocks is yellow; Summer Snow and Dogmar are white.

The Polyanthas list: Cameo, a light salmon color; Carol Ann, orange-pink; Cecile Brunner, light pink; George Elger, yellow; Gloria Mundi, orange-scarlet; Miss Edith Cavell, scarlet; and The Fairy, pink.

Among the Hybrid Perpetuals are listed: General Jacqueminot and Ulrich Brunner, both red to crimson; Baroness Rothschild, pink; and Frau Karl Druschki, white.

Shrub Roses are: Rosa Bugonis, yellow; Rosa Moyesii, red to crimson; Rosa Pomifera, pink; Harrison's Yellow, deep yellow, and Navada, white.

Miniature Roses are: Baby Gold Star, yellow; Midget, red; and Pixie, pale pink.

Ramblers list: Crimson Rambler, Crimson, and Excelsa, all red varieties; Hiawatha, red with a white eye; Dorothy Perkins, pink; White Dorothy, white; and Evangelene, rosy-white.

Among the Large Flowed Climbers are: Bess Lovett, red; Dr. W. Van Fleet, pink; City of York, white, Gardenia, yellow; and Jacotte, salmon and apricot.

Everblooming Climbers are: Blaze and Flash, both red; Dr. J. H. Nicolas and New Dawn, both pink; Mermaid and Mrs. Whitman Cross, both yellow and orange; and Penelope and Prosperity, both white.

Climbing Tea Roses are: Crimson Glory, red; Golden Dawn, yellow; Talisman, pink; and High Noon and Sungold, both yellow.

Climbing Polyanthas and Floribundas list: Goldilocks, yellow; Pinocchio, pink blend, and Pinkie, pink.

Note: Many of the names of roses are similar. Be sure to state the variety wanted as well as the name.

Lilacs

The old-fashioned lilac was two colors, white and purple. Today's lilacs are the result of experiment and change. Blossoms are larger, more colorful, and more fragrant. The French have been the leaders in development and many of the newer varieties bear French names. Many are hybrids, which is the grafting of specially-developed buds to common root stock. This is noticeable in a bulge just above the root. When planting keep the bulge at or slightly above ground level. If the hybrid should die the root will send up growth that will be either the common white or purple lilac.

Lilacs need full sunshine and rich, well-drained soil. Usually insects do not cause problems so there is no need for spraying with a pesticide. However mildew can become a problem in late summer. Mildew is a fungus, a parasitic plant growth that attaches itself to the leaf surface to grow and spread. Spraying preventatively with a fungicide can prevent the disease spreading, but once it gains a foothold it is difficult to destroy. It will not kill the lilac but may cause premature dropping of foliage if infestation is severe. Mildew is identified as a milky-white coating on the surface of the leaves. It is more common in hot moist weather.

Lilacs ordinarily grow ten to twelve feet in height but can grow as tall as twenty feet if competing with nearby trees. The lifespan is fifty years or more. Removing the expended flower stalks following blossoming enhances the beauty of the bush. If stalks are not removed they remain until the following spring and do not curtail that spring's blossoming.

If you wish to purchase the common white or common purple, ask for them by that term. If you wish hybrids the following are some that are available.

Belle de Nancy: rosy-pink with a white center.

Charles Jolly: dark double red.

Double Sweetheart: creamy coral pink.

Evangelene: fragrant lavender with red overtones.

George Bellair: reddish-purple.

Mme. Casimer Perier: fragrant double creamy white.

President Carnot: large light blue.

Thunberg: fragrant deep lavender with especially long stems.

Ludwig Spaeth: single deep purple.

James MacFarlane: a pink variety, very hardy, growing about eight feet tall.

Felty: a late blooming pink type.

Dwarf Korean: a small deep blue variety growing three to four feet in height.

Chinese: a compact low growing lilac with large reddish-purple blossoms.

Plant lilacs as singles or at five-foot spacing as hedges. Planting can be within three feet of buildings without harm to buildings or plants. Some French hybrids lack fragrance but make up for it in coloring and size.

Spiria behind a Barberry bush.

Close-up view of Spiria.

Spiria

Spiria is another old-fashioned plant that has been in use for many years. Its white blossom is one of the early flowers of spring. Growing to about a five-foot height, its flower-laden branches drop downward in graceful arching. It prefers sunlight but will grow in shade. It is not bothered by insects, nor by the cold of winter. Used as a hedge Spiria can give effective screening if planted four to five feet apart. Soil should be moderately dry and reasonably good. Once established it will continue giving pleasure to the eye for fifty years and more. I have grown three varieties, the Snowmound, Vanhouttei, and Bridal Wreath. All are white. Bridal Wreath is so named because the flowers tend to grow in parallel rows along the branches. The other two blossom more unevenly.

Spiria is usually purchased bare-rooted. It also comes balled and burlapped. Both give satisfactory planting. The following are other varieties and descriptions.

Reeves: a white variety growing as tall as eight feet. The blossoms are three to four times larger than most other varieties. Foliage is attractive.

Anthony Waterer: a dwarf plant about two feet tall with rose-red blossoms.

Pink Bouquet: a pink blossoming variety with flowers coming into bloom over an extended length of time.

Coccinea: another dwarf variety with red color that blossoms all summer.

Little Princess: a dwarf with pink blossoms.

A shrub known by two names—Rose of Sharon, and Althea.

A border of Althea of different colors.

Rose of Sharon

Rose of Sharon is also known by the name Althea. It is a tall growing bush that flowers in late summer. Althea is often planted closely to house foundations to screen chimneys, downspouts, etc. It also makes an attractive lawn tree that can be kept pruned to a desired height. If pruned at an early age it can become more like a bush than a tree. Foliage is dark green and attractive. Flowers can be either single or double depending on variety. Single flowers are a single row of petals surrounding the center; double is more than one row, sometimes several rows. The flower of Althea is about two inches in diameter, the petals crinkly with rounded corners, the colors are vivid, and flowering time is two weeks or more. Bushes can be purchased with multiple colored blossoms on the same bush. Late blooming varieties, such as Althea, generally are also late in the development of foliage in springtime. This bush is very hardy and will grow in all locations. Plant in well-drained soil, either in shade or full sunshine. Naturally it, like all flowering bushes, grows best in full sunshine. Insects pose no special problem but some fungi can attack in late summer. If yellowing occurs, spray with a fungicide spray. This bush, like others, is usually purchased bare rooted in a size of two to four feet tall. It is also sold as balled and burlapped. One can expect advancement of growth in a balled and burlapped shrub to be a full year ahead of a bare rooted one of the same size. The following are some of the more common varieties.

Hibiscus Syriacus: a single white flowering type.
Amplissimus: double red.
Arden's: double violet.
Jeanne d'Arc: double white.
Pulcherimus: double pink.
Multicolored: all of the above colors on one tree.

Honeysuckle

Honeysuckle can be either a bush or a vine. Both are hardy, both like full sunshine, and both will grow well in medium moist to dry soils. The vine is prolific and needs a trellis. The bushes vary in height depending on the variety; the average is approximately six feet. The flower is delicate looking—white, pink, or red depending on the variety—and is the favorite of the hummingbird, particularly in early morning. The foliage is attractive throughout the summer. The following are the more common varieties.

Everbloooming: a vine with flowers from late spring into late autumn. The flower is larger than most and bright red in color.

Halls Vine: a low-growing type that can be planted on steep banks to act as a ground cover, prevent erosion, curtail weed growth. It can be purchased as a pink, white, or a purple.

Zabeli's: a bush type with red foliage in early spring, bright red flowers, red fruit in autumn.

Arnold's Red: a fast growing variety that reaches eight feet tall. It is one of the best for exposed conditions. Flowers are deep crimson. Naturally, this one and all other bush type honeysuckle can be pruned to a lower height if desired.

Rubra Wheeling: a vigorous pink variety. The fruit, the size of small peas, is red.

Tartarian: can be either pink or white. Ask for it by color wanted.

Honeysuckle is generally purchased bare root. The size can vary according to the desire of the purchaser. I suggest a range of eighteen to forty-eight inches.

Forsythia in blossom.

Autumn coloring of White Dogwood.
In summer, its leaves are dark green.

Forsythia

Forsythia is the beautiful bright yellow flowering bush that literally glows in early spring. In preparing for the event the branching converts from green in winter to yellow in spring; the buds swell forth from every conceivable place to make the bush a mass of golden color. The one-inch-long, trumpet-shaped flowers last up to a full two weeks, then give way to foliage that arches downward in gentle curves. Forsythia grows to a height of about five feet and about the same in diameter. It grows best in dry soil, in full sunlight, and blossoms without fail unless buds are injured by severe winter temperatures. Indication of this is blossoms on branches that lay beneath snow cover while those more in the open remain bare.

Forsythia is a vigorous growing bush, and does require some pruning to keep it in shape. Prune after blossoming so as not to remove blossoming wood. It is usually purchased as a bare rooted plant in a two- to three-foot size. The following are some varieties available. In my opinion the quality is in the order listed. One feature all have in common, flower is yellow.

Lynnwood: a common variety of good quality.

Spring Glory: similar to Lynnwood.

Golden Bell: similar to Lynnwood and Spring Glory.

Tetragold: a low growing type valued more for foliage than blossom.

Weeping Forsythia: a thin limbed variety that arches downward.

Irish Golden Bell: a newer, more erect type recently imported from Ireland.

Dogwoods

Dogwood is a medium sized tree growing to approximately twenty-five feet. Its native home is the state of Missouri but it will grow in all but the coldest areas of the United States. Dogwood's use as a lawn tree should be limited to terrain protected either by surrounding wooded lots or buildings, and valleys with natural hillsides to offset winter's frigid air. Care must also be taken not to plant in too moist a soil. If it is too cold the trees will freeze back to ground level each year, sending up stems the following spring to revert to bush rather than tree. If it is too moist the saplings will simply die after a period of time. In the correct soil with adequate protection they make beautiful trees.

The Dogwood leaf is oval, approximately three inches long by two inches wide, sharply pointed with prominent veins. The delicate flower is unusual in having two pairs of petals opposite each other with dark lines in the center of each to, collectively, make the form of a cross. It can be red or white depending on variety. The top of each petal has a notch, and the tree trunk takes on a twisting appearance, giving certain credence to the legend that the cross on which Christ died was fashioned from dogwood. The only problem: Dogwood is an American tree which does not grow in north Africa.

Dogwood is named either Red or White, with the Red being the more expensive. Both the small seed that follow the blossom and the foliage turn a bright red in autumn as the tree prepares for cold weather. Rooting is extensive, tough to sever with a shovel, but balled and burlapped trees transplant well. As trees age the bark darkens to almost reddish-brown, separating by thin lines to form both round and square images that gives it an alligator-skin effect. The inner bark is said to be bitter tasting. It was boiled by the Indians as a cure for fevers, was used by early settlers for malaria, and by Southerners during the Civil War as a substitute for quinine. It was also used for dye. The strong wood is used in the making of golf club heads, mallets, chisel handles, and the like.

Dogwood appears to have no major insects. In the right terrain and climatic conditions it can be attractive and interesting to grow.

Flowering Quince in full bloom.

Flowering Quince

The Flowering Quince is a low growing bush with dense branching. The leaf is a shiny dark green, attractive in summer, and a dull red in autumn. Blossoming in very early spring, the bright red flowers—about one and one half inches in diameter—stand out like lights on a Christmas tree. The flowers pollinate to produce apple-sized fruits that are used in a number of ways, particularly for making quince jelly. Growing to a four- to five-foot height, Quince hugs the ground to discourage both grass and weeds from growing under its spread of branching. It grows best in good soil, in full sunlight. Attacking insects are few. Used to protect corners of lots subjected to foot travel, it lives on for many years with need for only minor care.

More Bushes

Before concluding my description on interesting bushes I want to add a few that I am not currently growing but have grown in the past.

Butterfly Bush is an enticingly named bush that disappointed me. It might be suitable for hedging, but neither the leaf nor white flower attracted butterflies more than any other flowering bush. I believe there is also a pink flowering variety.

Redozier Dogwood is another disappointing bush that has a limited place in landscaping. Its white flower does resemble White Dogwood's, as does the leaf, but it grows as a weed bush in many moist areas of New York State, perhaps in other states as well. It is quite attractive with its bright red stems in early spring, the ease with which it is transplanted, and screening effect, for hydrants and electrical boxes, for which it can be used.

Burning Bush, or Euonymus, is used almost exclusively in the dwarf variety for landscaping. This brilliantly red-leafed bush can be used for hedging or singly. Its red coloring is primarily pre-winter coloring but foliage is attractive also during the summer. It grows best in well drained soils of rich texture to a height of five to six feet with a diameter approximately the same. American Euonymus grows to ten feet in height, the Winged to twenty feet, but neither are often used as lawn trees. Use care when ordering to ensure the right variety.

Flowering Almond is a delicate looking but hardy shrub with masses of small pink blossoms in early May. It grows to about three feet in height.

Snowball is of Japanese origin. It is a long-lived bush that grows to eight feet tall and about the same in width. The blossoms start out as hydrangea do, small green balls that grow to baseball size with white miniature flowers. Soil needs to be rich and well drained.

Barberry is another Japanese type of low growing bush. Its small glossy leaves turn to red in autumn. The white flowers convert to red oblong fruits that hang on the branching throughout the winter. The branches are hard textured, red in coloring, and thorny with very sharp thorns. The life span is well past fifty years.

Hedging

My dictionary describes a hedge as a fence or boundary formed by a dense row of shrubs or low trees. In recent years, because of the proximity of housing and the installation of swimming pools both above and below ground, hedging materials are in demand. Just as care must be taken to plant trees and shrubs in soils conducive to obtaining good growth, care must also be taken when planting hedges. In addition the type of plantings must be carefully considered. Some are deciduous, and so lose their screening properties when foliage drops. Some are considered to be dirty, dropping debris at times. Some fruit to drop ripened fruits on sidewalks and driveways, some grow wider than desired. Some grow tall and lose their lower leaves, and thus defeat the purpose. I hope to explain several types of hedge materials to assist the reader in making a judgment.

Arborvitie is an evergreen often used as a hedge. There are many varieties of Arborvitie but the one used most often in hedging is the upright American. Its good qualities are that it grows reasonably fast, approximately twelve inches per season, that it is narrow, approximating a five foot width, that it grows well in both dry and moist soils, and that its lifespan is long. It retains most of its foliage all year long and holds that foliage at lower levels no matter how closely plants are spaced. The normal spacing is two, three, or four feet. It can be topped at any desired height at any time of the year without injury. It will grow double stems, or triple stems, often when grown from seed. These can be left to grow or cut off close to the ground level to produce a single plant. Because stems are slender in new plantings supports may be needed to prevent breakage from icing in winter, or the plants can be topped somewhat to produce thicker trunks. Arborvitie is normally free of disease. I have not had to spray any plants with either pesticide or fungicide.

The bad qualities, if they can be termed that, are that about fifty percent of trees over two feet in height develop clusters of seeds that slowly turn a brown color as they ripen in autumn. The seeds fall to the ground during winter and some grow to produce more plants. Arborvitie is a member of the pine family. It has the same habit of converting from deep green to dull brown as cold weather approaches. It also sheds last season's foliage, as pines do last season's needles, the inner leaves turning brown very suddenly to dry and drop from the branching.

Plants that are not topped will grow to about eighteen feet. The root system is extensive, making it easy to dig and transplant. I consider it an important plant in landscaping.

Another plant in demand for hedges is Olive. This silvery-leafed, thorny plant is more tree than bush. Autumn Olive is a denser, more bush-like looking than its cousin the Russian Olive. The Autumn produces more fruits than the Russian, fruits that are feed for both birds and squirrels just prior to winter. Both are considered to be dirty plants as the dropped fruits do litter areas beneath the trees. Both need severe top pruning to maintain hedge-like appearance as foliage tends to move upward on unpruned plants, exposing supporting trunk surfaces. Both grow rapidly, three to four feet yearly, growing best in relatively dry soils. Both are deciduous. Both grow five to six feet in width. A good hedge material in the proper setting.

Privet comes in three varieties, two originating in China and the third a California strain. All three are deciduous but retain leaves far into cold weather. The California strain tends to have a larger leaf and grow wider. Privets are like Arborvitie in growing habit, tall and narrow with foliage at the bottom dense regardless of closeness of plants. The usual distance for planting is one to two feet. This strong, woody plant will grow to about ten feet if not topped. It can be topped at any time of year and at any desired height. The leaf is small, averaging about one inch in length, with a scattering of white blossoms during the early summer. It is very hardy, tops dying only if temperatures drop to twenty below zero. Even then if tops are removed at ground level roots will grow new growth, the severing to be done in early spring. Privet requires dry soil and will not grow in moist areas.

The two China varieties, North Amur and South Amur, are similar in hardiness and growing habit. Plants are usually purchased in a twelve- to twenty-four-inch size, the root inserted into the soil to the same depth it was originally planted. Water weekly the first growing season and, of course, the ideal planting time for all new plantings is the month of April.

Most of the flowering bushes can be hedging if width is not a problem. Spiria, Mock Orange, Forsythia, and Weigela can be used separately or intermixed. Rose of Sharon, or Althea as it is often called, can make a narrow hedge if used by itself. The many colors available make it especially attractive when in blossom.

Evergreens, including Colorado Blue Spruce and other varieties, make an attractive dense hedge in a single row. It is wise to use a single variety as growing patterns differ. Planting a double or triple row prevents sunlight from the inner and lower branching, causing needle loss and thus exposing bare wood. This loss of lower branching is seen when viewing blocks of machine-planted trees.

Naturally, rows of Birch, Maple, or other type of deciduous tree can be used as a tall hedge.

Deciduous Trees

A deciduous tree is one that sheds its leaves during cold weather. Pin Oaks retain dead leaves and stems until they are pushed off by new growth in early spring. Pin Oaks are deciduous trees. Larch is similar to evergreen in summer but drops all needles in late autumn. It is deciduous. Some plants retain leaves all through cold weather. Euonymus is such a plant. It is considered evergreen even though its leaves are the flat variety. North and South Amur Privet retain leaves until mid-winter. Both are spoken of as being deciduous. Deciduous trees do not become dormant until leaves fall. Consequently the dormant season is shorter than for evergreens. In the northeastern United States the dormant period begins shortly after several light frosts or a single severe one. The date is about mid-October. Trees can then be dug and replanted safely until warm weather promotes new growth in April, perhaps into early May. As with all nursery stock, the growing of plants in containers or the heeling in of previously dug and burlapped stock, extends the season for planting.

A pink flowering Crabapple, probably Almy variety.

A Thundercloud Purple Leaf Plum. Injured Arborvitie in background—probably due to careless herbicide use.

Crabapples

The building of new homes has created a demand for trees that beautify in addition to offering shade. Among these are Crabapples. Crabapples have been developed to enhance property greatly without the litter of dropped fruit that was prevalent only short years ago. Today's trees blossom profusely and yield fruits of insignificant size. But Crabapple trees are apple trees and need the same kinds of well drained soils as do the common apples. They are also subject to the same damage by insects and mice. Since the fruits, except in the case of Dolga which is large enough to be used in the making of apple jelly, are not consumed by humans the need for spraying is lessened.

Crabapples grow in various sizes, with different colored blossoms and differences in leaf coloring. Problems caused by mice, and how to prevent them are written up in detail in the description of home orchards. The second most annoying pest is web worms, those web-spinning green worms that infest trees to feed on foliage. Part of prevention is searching for egg masses that adhere to wool branching in late autumn. The egg mass is a square inch size of closely bound eggs. It is dry to the touch and easily pried from the branch. Dispose of them by allowing them to fall to the ground, or by other means. It is by no means certain that worms will infest your tree; not all trees become infested.

Varieties of Crabapple are numerous. The following are types that I have grown and consider to be among the best.

Eleyi: a small tree growing from ten to twelve feet tall and about the same in width. Unopened buds are bright red but open to reddish-purple. Blossoms grow in clusters to completely cover the tree. Fragrance is very sweet. Foliage is bright red in early summer, turning a darker red as summer progresses. Fruits are the size of marbles, bright red when ripe. The red fruits attract birds and many are eaten before falling to the ground.

Hopa: pronounced "hope-a". A larger tree growing up to twenty feet, with spread of branching about fifteen feet. Blossom is pink with white center. First leaves are tinged with red but revert to all green after blossoms fade.

Radiant: a Crabapple with branching sweeping upward to give it a narrower shape and increased density. Buds are rose-red opening to bright red. Radiant grows to fifteen feet in height.

Almy: a smaller variety growing to twelve feet. Blossoms are deep red with white centers.

Purple Wave: another small variety with red leaves and red blossoms. Foliage retains color all summer long.

Straphmore: a narrow variety growing twelve to fifteen feet. Blossom is reddish-pink.

Some additional Crabapples are Flame, Calloway, and Washington, all with white blossoms. Van Eseltine, Floribunda, and Katherine are all pink. Royality, Profusion, and Liset, are all red blooming.

Note: The color of blossoms can be easily seen when trees are in blossom but color can also be determined to a degree when trees are dormant. Red or purple blossoming trees generally have darker wood, while pink and white blossoming trees have various shades of gray in trunk in branching. Breaking off a branch in red and purple crabs show the same coloring within the deeper wood. White and pink crabs do not indicate interior coloring. Wood that is hard, as indicated by the pressure needed on handles of pruning shears to cut comparable thickness of branch, means blossoming will be late while the reverse indicates early blossoming.

Purple Leaf Plum

Purple Leaf Plum is a small plum tree noted for its tiny white blossom and bright red leaf. It is an upland tree with reddish-tan wood. The blossom is fragrant and fills the surrounding air with its sweet aroma in early spring. The fruit is plum shaped, about half an inch in length and a quarter inch in diameter. It turns red when ripe. Trees grow to normal size for plum trees, eight to ten feet in height and six to eight feet in diameter of branching. It is subject to damage by saw fly worms in much the same manner as are Crabapples. Control is by spraying with pesticide upon discovering infection. Most Purple Plums can go a lifetime without the need for spraying. Because of its small size it can be planted within three feet of building foundations. Plant only in well drained soils.

Thundercloud is a variety that retains its bright red leaf color all through the summer.

Newport begins as a red leaf in early spring but converts to a green-leafed tree when warmer weather arrives. Both grow at the same rate and to the same size.

Honey Locust tree.

Green Weeping Willow.

Locusts

Locusts are trees having compound leaves, long stems with pairs of leaflets along the sides and directly opposite one another. Foliage is a light green that lets sunlight filter through to give what is called light shade. Locusts are upland trees requiring dry soils. Most varieties grow thirty to forty feet tall with a top span of about thirty feet. The Sunburst is a newer variety which grows more upright than the Shademaster, Honey, and other varieties. Locusts described here are free of thorns, need dry soils, and are hard-wooded trees that live for fifty years or more. Some can become infested with wood borers that are deep within the wood and almost impossible to control. Fortunately such infestation is rare. In late summer web worms appear to select locust trees in which to build nests of unsightly webbing that do little harm except to the trees' beauty. If the nests are within reach a pesticide spray will destroy the developing worms. Spray at dusk when feeding worms are more likely to be back in the nest.

Honey Locust is the more common and least expensive variety. It also grows the tallest. In early spring the sweet odor of pendulant flowers fills the air. The blossoms convert to seeded pods that hang on branches until autumn, then both seeds and pods separate to fall to the ground.

Moraine is a podless type with darker leaf. It grows rapidly to reach heights of thirty to forty feet with an umbrella-shaped top. It is considered a good lawn tree.

Shademaster grows less tall than the Marine. Its foliage gives the appearance of hemlock evergreen. Bark is smooth, growth rapid.

Sunburst is a new variety that lacks chlorophyll in new growth, which accentuates the contrast between older and newer to give the appearance of sunlit tips, thus the name. It is also podless.

There are other varieties in addition to those named.

Willows

Willows are trees that will grow in very wet soils and also in dry soils. The most commonly used ones are American, Wisconsin, Green, Niobe, Golden, and Corkscrew. All are large trees. In addition there are several types of low growing bushes called Pussy Willows. Anyone wishing to start a willow can do so by cutting off a branch the thickness of one's thumb. Cut off an eight-inch length and shove it down into wet soil at a forty-five degree angle. Be sure the buds face upward. In time the upper buds will begin to grow, while the lower buds beneath ground develop into roots. When the upward shoots reach twenty-four to thirty-six inches in length, dig the willow, cut off all upward growth excepting one, and replant. You will now gain a willow tree.

A willow whistle, a delight to both boys and girls, can be made from early spring willow. Cut a segment the thickness of an inch or less, about five inches in length. Cut a vee-shaped groove in the wood about two inches from one end. At about two and a half inches from the same end cut the bark deep enough to free it, cutting a circle to girdle the segment. With a twisting motion to and fro loosen the bark to slide it from the inner wood. Cut a flat from the groove to the end of the inner wood and taper the end to increase the pressure when forcing air through the opening. Slide the cylinder back on the inner wood and blow on the tapered end. You now have a penetrating whistle.

Willows are attractive from a distance but have unpleasant characteristics as well. The trailing branches often reach the ground and interfere with lawn work. Mosquitoes frequent the thick branches to emerge at nightfall. The trailing branches cannot always sustain themselves, and portions die to fall from the tree in strong wind, particularly in springtime. Rooting is extensive and shallow, which makes cutting grass beneath the trees more difficult. Regardless, it is often planted as a lawn tree in the expectation it will absorb water and dispense it into the air. Most trees do this but none quite efficiently as the willow.

American is a straight-trunked tree found in natural settings along creek banks and nature's wet areas. It is a large tree with an average trunk diameter of thirty-six inches and a height of fifty to seventy feet at maturity. It is not a weeping type.

Wisconsin is a weeping type with dark green foliage and bark. It grows straight and rapidly in moist soils. It grows as large as the American with branches trailing downward due to the weight of the long, narrow, dark green leaves.

Niobe is similar to Wisconsin, except the trailing branches are more slender.

Golden is a yellow-barked variety. The yellow fades out somewhat with the onset of cold winter weather but brightens in early spring. Golden grows more irregularly than others but leaf size, weeping habit, and size of tree compares to others.

Corkscrew is an unusual variety with support wood growing in gentle curves to form the effect from which it gets its name. It is not the massive tree as are other willows. The leaf, however, is similar. It is not a weeping type.

Pussy Willows are to standard trees what shrubs are to deciduous trees. Most grow eight to ten feet in height and grow as bushes with multiple stems. In the wild Pussy Willows are found in the same general locations as are the large willows. Catkins are prelude to blossoms, the blossom being an inch-long cylinder surrounded by small projection flowers. The catkins can vary in size and coloring. The so-called pink are white catkins that turn reddish on the sunlight side before they become blossoms.

Complaints concerning Pussy Willows range from excessive growth to attack by scale or insects to attraction for bees in late autumn. All the complaints are valid. Pussy Willow is a vigorous growing shrub that requires pruning from time to time. They can be pruned at any time of year and in the amount the owner desires. Scale is an ongoing problem. Watch for elongated white specks on the exterior of the bark, not on the foliage, and if detected spray once with a dormant oil. One application is all that is required for control if the mixture is correct and the weather remains dry for a twenty-four hour period. Insects that attack all willows, both Pussies and trees, are dark feeding worms produced by what is known as the Cloak Butterfly; spray to wet the worms with a pesticide. In late autumn bees are attracted to Pussy Willows to feed on sap released from foliage by aphids. Aphids are difficult to see with the naked eye, but bothersome bees are indication of their presence. Spraying with a pesticide will eliminate the aphids and the bees will no longer be attracted. In severe cases of scale or aphids, cut willows to ground level which permits new growth. Disposing of the old growth disposes of the insects as well.

A Tuliptree about twenty years old.

The unusual leaf of the Tuliptree.

Tuliptree

I write about the Tuliptree with mixed emotions. It is an attractive shade tree, a tree that excites curiosity both for its unusual leaf and its straw-like cup seed flowers. It is considered a warm climate tree but does grow as far north as the northern United States. I first discovered this tree growing in the woods which border on my nursery. Further investigation disclosed a number of both old and new saplings growing in neighboring wooded areas also. Obtaining permission, I dug a couple of dozen, some of which I sold to customers and some I replanted in the nursery. The ones I planted in the nursery grew quite well. All but one of the dozen or so that I sold died, and I was obligated to replace each with a different type but comparably priced tree. I must add that the ones I grew in the nursery were eventually sold also, and most survived the two replantings. I do not know the reason for failure in the one instance and success in the other.

Tuliptree is a tall straight tree that grows best in moderately moist soil. I do not know if the name reflects the tulip-shaped silhouette of the leaf or the tulip-shaped straw flowers. The leaf is a heavy weight, dark green in summer, with the far edge giving the impression of being cut straight by shearing. The autumn color is yellow, and foliage falls from the tree at the first light frost. The straw cups remain throughout the winter.

Tuliptrees have tap roots, a strong textured carrot-like root that, because of its depth, needs to be severed in digging and burlapping the ball. Normally, the cutting off of tap roots on trees does not interfere with successful transplanting.

A beautiful and attractive tree when successfully planted.

Paul's Scarlet Hawthorn in full splendor.

Closer view of Hawthorn in flowering stage.

Hawthorn

I must admit my knowledge of Hawthorn is limited. I have grown only the one variety, Paul's Scarlet. It is crimson red. Another variety, Washington, is white. My several dozen Hawthorns are sold and, hopefully, growing well in some homeowner's yard. All were sold before blossoming so I will have to draw on description of a Paul's Scarlet growing in my own yard. I love this tree and am sorry that it is growing old. It is more bush than tree, having several stems from a point of branching close to ground level. I do not know the reason for it being a bush as it was twelve to fifteen feet tall when we purchased it in 1940. Every spring without fail it has burst forth in late May with the colorful red blossoms that characterize Paul's Scarlet. The blossoms grow in clusters, each less than an inch in diameter, resembling a dandelion in texture but crimson red with a white center. The odor is insignificant, as are the small white seeds produced by the flower, but the beauty lasts almost two full weeks. The leaf resembles the Irish shamrock; it is bright green and, like the flowers, small. This tree is an upland tree requiring dry soil. Being a long-lived tree, the wood is very dense and hard, and is studded with inch-long thorns. I am always surprised that birds invariably build nests high up in the branching regardless of the thorny interior. At present the tree is about thirty feet in height and growth has slowed to only inches per season.

About ten years ago my tree began suffering from mildew. Mildew is a parasitic plant that grows on leaf surface, particularly in hot moist weather. It draws moisture from the leaf and ultimately causes the leaf to dehydrate and fall from the tree. Infestation can be serious or not. Control is by spraying with a fungicide in a preventative measure. After mildew becomes established, control becomes more difficult. Infested trees may lose foliage as early as mid-August but other than that damage is minor. Trees will leaf out the following spring and blossom fully as usual. This single tree indicates that the Scarlet lives long beyond sixty years. I assume the Washington also is long-lived.

A Little Leaf Linden in a front yard.

Closer view of Linden leaves.

Linden

Linden is a tree valued for its wood in the making of ladders. The reason is it's both lightweight and strong. It grows in the wild as a large tree with large leaves. The leaf is oval shaped, perhaps as large as six by eight inches. In landscaping the smaller leafed relative called the Little Leaf Linden is sometimes used as a lawn tree.

The leaf of the Little Leaf is about two and a half by three and a half inches. It is a heavy-bodied, bright green leaf, with a darker shade of green on top and more silvery color underneath. It grows as tall as sixty-five feet with a top spread of branching about twenty to twenty-five feet in diameter. In early spring trees take on unusual enlarged buds that turn a cherry red, buds that develop into small white fragrant flowers. Soils for the Linden can be moist to dry. The root is comparably shallow, soft to cut with a digging shovel, which is usual in soft-wooded trees.

The need for spraying the Little Leaf is minimal. Occasionally brown circular patches appear on leaf surfaces distracting from beauty of the tree, but the damage is not a lasting one. Wood in saplings is smooth but the texture roughens as trees mature.

A young Red Bud tree in a neighboring yard.

Close-up look at Red Bud foliage.

Red Bud

The Red Bud is a colorful tree growing to a forty- to fifty-foot height. It is an upland tree with deep penetrating roots. The wood is both strong and hard. This tree is said to be related to the Pea family but for the life of me I don't know if it's the garden pea or some other pea. That is immaterial. What is important is that it, literally, becomes covered with delicate pink blossoms prior to the emergence of leaves. The blossoms seem to spring out of structural wood, out of branching wood and end twigs. Thus they become a mass of solid color. In time the blossoms give way to foliage, heart-shaped leaves three to five inches long by three to four inches wide. The color is a deep green, and lower branches retain foliage as the tree grows. I am told that pods result from the blossoms to ripen and be discarded in late July and August. I have not kept any that long a time in my nursery.

Information has it that the blossoms are sometimes used as food, being mixed into salads. The red root can yield a dye. This tree appears to be hardy, withstanding temperature to twenty below zero. I recommend it as a yard tree.

European Mountain Ash in my nursery.

Close-up view of Ash fruits.

Mountain Ash

Books inform me that the Mountain Ash is not an ash, that it belongs to the Rowen variety, another type of tree. Most associate it with the several ash varieties including the Red, Blue, Black, and Green, that are grown for timber.

Mountain Ash is an upland tree that grows best in a well-drained soil. If the site is too moist a tree will survive but fail to grow. Often the foliage looks unhealthy. Normally Mountain Ash will grow rapidly. I purchased a quantity of eighteen-inch-tall trees one spring and sold them two years later at heights of from six to eight feet. Healthy Mountain Ash grow to about twenty-five feet in height with a top spread of ten to fifteen feet. Spring blossoms are white, converting to green fruit which turns brilliant crimson in autumn. All trees contain both male and female components and thus all produce berries. The so-called berries are miniature apple-type fruits that are consumed by birds, which sometimes become intoxicated from overindulgence.

The leaf of the Mountain Ash is compound, a single long stem with pairs of leaflets opposite one another. Damage by insects is minimal, usually worms similar to those by saw flies which feed on foliage. A single spraying with a pesticide is the usual method for control.

Three White Birch clumps, approximately ten years old, blowing in a strong wind.

A mature White Birch of the European variety, age about twenty-five years of age.

White Birch

Birch is one of the popular lawn trees. Like Maple, Birch has adapted to soil conditions separating highland and lowland trees. There are many kinds of birch, such as Black, River, and Yellow, that are not commonly used in landscaping. The four varieties that are in demand are Gray, European, Paper, and Weeping. Each one is different from the other but the one thing in common is white bark.

Gray is a misleading name for a White Birch as it gives the impression of gray instead of white. Perhaps the reason is differences in the shades of whiteness among the Grays. All Birch start out as brown-skinned saplings with very short vertical lines dotting the surface. As the sapling increases in age and size it begins to lighten at the base and the change to white is gradual, slowly moving up as the tree grows. Some Grays begin the whitening process earlier than others and so some appear to be gray by contrast. Not all Birch gain the white flaking bark that is admired. In mature Grays the white bark divides to form dark-lined, diamond-shaped islands beginning, as the whiteness began earlier, at the base and moving upward.

Gray is a wetland birch that will grow in heavy clay soils. It is shallow rooted; the wood is soft and easily cut with a digging shovel. It transplants easily and grows quickly, except it does not transplant well in autumn unless watering is frequent. Gray grows to about twenty-five feet tall with a top spread of ten to fifteen feet. The autumn color is solid yellow. Because Gray is fast growing it lends itself to clumping, that is the growing of more than one stem from a common site. I say site instead of root because there are two methods used to start clumps. One method is to cut a vigorous young birch off at ground level in early spring and, as new growth grows from the root, to select two or three stems to form a clump while the remaining shoots are cut off. A second method is to simply plant two or three saplings in the same site. Growing stems from a common root insures that the characteristics of foliage are identical, while planting several individual trees in a common site can mean subtle differences in leaf structure.

European Birch is an upland tree that will tolerate considerable moisture but does not grow well in heavy clay. It is a larger tree than the Gray, growing to forty to fifty feet tall with a top spread of twenty to thirty feet. It grows as quickly as the Gray, and has dark tan bark that does not whiten until saplings reach heights of twelve to fifteen feet. The branching is not as dense as the Gray's, but leaves are larger and appear not to be as subject to injury as is the Gray. The bark of mature trees is very white and smooth to the touch. European can be clumped if desired but because of size is more often planted as single. The root is a spreading one, quite shallow, and digging for transplanting usually is successful.

Paper Birch, so named because of the thin paper-like bark that peels from its exterior, is an upland tree. It grows very tall, very slender, and is the whitest of all the birches. Particularly nice specimens grow on the land side of lakes in the Adirondack mountains. Whether planted by humans, or growing naturally, they tower along the shores leaning outward as if to peer into the depths. The height of the Paper, plus its unique characteristic of clinging layers of dry bark, are the only differences between it and the Gray. The autumn color is bright yellow, as are all birches'.

I have not grown Weeping Birch but am familiar with it. Weeping is a type of European with some characteristics of the weeping willow. The growth is slower than the regular European but mature size is comparable. Weeping is an upland tree with a life span of fifty to seventy-five years. The spread of branching in mature trees is about twenty-five feet.

Birches are subject to damage by the Birch miner. This winged insect can be seen with the naked eye, flying over and around birch, if one looks up against the evening sky in early June. The leaf is pierced and eggs deposited between the leaf layers. The young feed on chlorophyll, leaving bare patches that, while partly destroying beauty, will not destroy the tree. Control is by spraying prior to infestation, one of the few preventative sprays I recommend, and continued spraying at weekly intervals through the month of June. Control is also obtained by applying a systemic pesticide in early spring. Spread it evenly on the ground surface in a circle around the tree as large as the outline of branching. This pesticide is available in garden stores. Follow directions and use caution. Most systemics require being driven deeper into the soil by watering.

Borers are worms that bore through the bark at ground level and then bore upward while feeding on the cambium layer. Heavy infestation can kill a tree but it is not likely to be that serious. Most trees can outgrow the damage caused by one or two borers, except when aging or becoming unhealthy for other reasons. Borers in a diseased tree are not always the cause for the tree dying.

Application of herbicides to lawns adversely affects all trees, and Birch in particular. My opinion is that Birches root shallow and thus are more likely to absorb a herbicide. I learned this by chance. Unwanted bushes grow in nurseries such as mine, and to destroy them I use a herbicide. I discovered that whenever I sprayed close to a birch, even though I was careful not to spray the tree itself, it would invariably die. I have also learned, in a different way, that newly planted trees will die if in the path of surface runoff water that has been contaminated with herbicide. I pass along this warning to others.

Pin Oak, about fifteen years old, in autumn color.

Oaks

Information from a reliable source states that there are more than sixty types of Oaks. Most are large trees used mainly for timber. The Scarlet is a wild tree which grows in wooded areas and turns bright red in autumn. The one most used in landscaping is the Pin Oak. It has a dull red autumn color, a drooping appearance in branching, and leaves that refuse to drop until pushed off by the new season's developing buds. Why should such a tree be used as a lawn tree? Possibly for the described reasons. Pin Oaks grow upward to eighty feet tall with rather narrow branch spread. There appears to be no strong leader, yet the trees manage to gain height. Lower branches point downward, leaves are long and narrow with needle-like projections to the sides. Color is bright green during summer. Trees produce small acorns, about half an inch in diameter and less than a quarter inch in height. Acorns are characteristic brown with shallow saucers.

Pin Oak is an upland tree and requires dry soil to grow well. The wood in young trees is dark-colored and smooth, in mature trees dark and rough-barked. Roots are tough to cut with a digging shovel and go deeply into the ground. In spite of this most dig well for transplanting.

Some additional oaks are: Bur, Chestnut, White, Northern Red, Black, Water, and Willow.

Destructive insects are gypsy moth, web worms, and certain types of fungi. The gypsy is curtailed by wrapping the trunk of the tree with burlap or plastic, binding it tightly with cord or wire, and folding the wrapping down over the tie. This prevents developing caterpillars from climbing the tree to feed on its foliage. There is no specific method to control web worms other than by burning their nests with fire or spraying each with a pressurized spray, or removing them by hand if they are within reach. Fungi are identified by the darkening of the normally dark green bark to a blotched gray look that gives the appearance of deadness. Control is spraying bark with a fungicide; several sprays may be necessary if the tree, or trees, are badly infected. Most trees grow without damage from fungi, and web worms are temporary pests that do only minor damage. An interesting and attractive lawn tree.

Sugar Maples planted by me in our yard. Both are thirty years old.

Close-up of Sugar Maple leaf.

*Silver Maple in foreground is from my nursery.
It was one and a half inch caliper plus eight feet tall
when planted four years ago.*

Close-up of Silver Maple leaves.

Norway Male in a town park. Estimated age is twenty-five years. Note rounded top.

Crimson King Red Leaf Maple, grown in my nursery, at twenty years of age. This picture does not give justice to its bright red coloring.

The Maple Family

When one is reminded of maple trees thoughts may vary. To one it's cool shade on hot summer days. To another the thought is of leaves to gather and dispose of in late autumn. Another may be reminded of products like maple syrup or maple sugar. To the more romantic it's the fall coloring of foliage in its blend of red and yellows. Maples are very important trees in landscaping.

Maples grow in the wild as easily as they grow on the lawns of countless individuals. They have adapted to different soil conditions and different climatic conditions. In addition, nurseries have made changes in developing Red Leaf trees. The more common maples—Sugar, Silver, Scarlet, Norway, and Sycamore—are easy to identify. Red Leaf maples such as Crimson King, Royality, and Faassens, are quite similar as most are budded to Norway stock to retain the size of that particular variety. Schwedler starts out in springtime as red-leafed but turns to green during the summer. Uncommon maples are Striped, Mountain, Siberian, Florida, Black, and Hedge. I will describe the more common.

Sugar is the one maple with sufficient sugar in its sap to make syrup and maple sugar. Forty to fifty gallons of sap are required to produce one gallon of syrup. Evaporation of the syrup produces sugar. The sap is collected very early in spring when it is pressured by the roots to rise to feed developing buds. The collection period lasts about two weeks and varies greatly due to weather.

Sugar is a large tree growing upwards to 100 feet with a trunk diameter of three to five feet. It is deeply rooted, long lived, and has hard-grained wood. It grows only in upland, well-drained soils. Its top spread can be sixty feet; it will grow with branching intertwined with another similar tree at as close as ten feet spacing, but normal spacing is forty to sixty feet. The leaf is large, five inches in diameter, sometimes pointed, long stems, with red and yellow autumn coloring. Single-winged seed clusters can hang heavily on female trees. In young trees the bark is smooth with dark gray color, but older trees develop deep grooves vertical to the trunk. Because Sugars grow tall saplings will normally grow upward rapidly before beginning to branch outward. This outward growth can be hastened by cutting off the tops of young, ten to twelve feet tall, trees. Cut off approximately three feet of upward growth but refrain from cutting below a grouping of outward-formed branching.

Sugar is identified by a knowledge of its leaf, by its growing site which is always high land, and by needle-sharp points at the ends of the branching. Also end twigs are small in diameter, usually about a quarter inch. Leaf stems will tear from the wood when forced to do so.

Insects of the Sugar are several, gypsy moth caterpillars the more recent one. Control is by wrapping the trunk with burlap or plastic, binding it tightly with string or wire, then folding the upper section downward to cover the binding. Caterpillars crawling upward become trapped and can easily be destroyed. The maple trumpet worm was very numerous in the mid-eighties but, like may infestations, lasted only a short time. This bright green, fast-moving worm, which is about an eighth of an inch in diameter and a half inch in length, protects itself doubly. Attaching itself to the underside of a leaf with webbing it folds the leaf over a trumpet-like enclosure into which it retreats when in danger. The double protection makes it very difficult to gain control. Fortunately for humans Nature appears to have done the job effectively. It is no longer a problem. In addition to these, numerous feeding insects take a bite or two from leaves; none poses a problem to the tree's survival.

Norway is a maple requiring the same type of upland site as the Sugar. It is not as massive a tree, growing to fifty feet tall with a top spread of about forty feet. Its green leaf is slightly larger than the Sugar's, and the stem wraps halfway around the end branches to bleed a white mucous sap when torn loose. It is the only maple to bleed. Slow growing, like the Sugar, its wood is hard and its lifespan long. The autumn coloring is unvaried, a pumpkin yellow. Seed pods on female trees are double-winged and numerous. In spite of this it is a desirable lawn tree. I might add that branching is more dense than the Sugar because the Norway's stance is more horizontal than the upright Sugar.

Scarlet and Silver are similar in several ways. Both are wetland trees, both grow rapidly, both have green summer foliage, and both have red twig ends on branching. Scarlet is also called by its Latin name, *Acer Rubrum*, by the common name of Swamp Maple, and Scarlet due to its bright red autumn coloring. That coloring varies from tree to tree and is more pronounced when autumn brings a series of non-killing frosts.

The Scarlet's leaf is round shaped with shallow points, while the Silver's is longer than it is wide and has deep points. The rapid growth indicates light wood lacking the strength of either the Norway or Sugar. However, if one is careful to avoid trees with sharp crotches in the upward growth, both make very satisfactory lawn trees. Both, like all wetland trees, have shallow but extensive root systems. Scarlet is identified by its site in growing, by its leaf during the summer, by red hanging flowers in early spring, and by autumn color. In my opinion the Scarlet is a stronger wooded tree than the Silver.

Silver is so named because of a silvery sheen on the underside of the foliage that becomes noticeable when leaves are upturned in wind. It has little fall color, although some trees will show some red. Both the Scarlet and Silver grow to fifty or sixty feet in height with a forty- to fifty-foot top spread.

Sycamore is another maple that grows best in wet soils but often grows well in highlands. It is noted for its greenish and whitish patches of bark on trunks of mature trees. The leaves are large, deep green in summer with little autumn color. A small white flower produces button-like seeds, so the tree is sometimes called a buttonwood tree. In recent years a bacteria has infested buds to destroy many, so spring foliage is scant. The trees usually recover during the summer. These large trees give both shade and beauty for upwards of 100 years.

The three Red Leaf maples named previously are generally budded onto a Norway root stock and consequently have the same characteristics as a growing Norway. The Crimson King was patented by number 735 in Germany a long time ago. Royality, I was told, was developed by Kelly's Nursery in Dansville, New York. They have discontinued business. I do not know the origin of Faassens. Of the three I consider the Crimson the best.

More Trees

In limiting my description to trees grown in my nursery I am, possibly, neglecting others of importance. If an individual likes a variety of tree, that variety becomes important. A nursery is limited by two considerations: will a particular variety grow, or will it sell if it will grow? Some of the following I did grow for a short time. Some I observed from a distance but did not grow. There are some I wished I had planted, but for some reason or other, didn't. A description will be brief.

Tree of Heaven: a medium tree growing to thirty or forty feet high. Some do grow taller. Fast growing with large leaves, it bears small clusters of yellow flowers in late June. Like the Locust, seeds develop in pods that cling to branching all summer and fall to the ground in autumn. The long stems that support the pods also fall to create more litter. It is claimed this tree will grow in all types of soils.

Smoke Tree: an American tree related to Sumac. My observation is that it is more likely a bush than a tree. Wood is yellow and said to give off an unpleasant odor when broken. Leaves are wide with blunt tips. Foliage turns to a brilliant red in fall. The name comes from the tree's clusters of feathery fruits that resemble puffs of wood smoke. Trunks can be as large as twelve inches in diameter.

Magnolia: an early flowering tree growing from small to thirty feet. Varieties are Bigleaf, Earleaf, Cucumber, Umbrella, and Saucer. The Magnolia is a southern tree with one variety, the Saucer, that grows well in the northern United States. The Saucer grows twelve to fourteen feet, has large leaves, and develops showy, fist-sized pink-

and-white blossoms. Large brownish fruits follow the blossom, the outer shell of which dry when ripe. The pods open at intervals to release seeds attached to silken threads.

Catalpa: a tree with very large leaves, growing up to twenty feet. The eight-inch wide by twelve-inch long leaves are light green. In spring dangling flowers, white with yellow and purple spots, give off a sweet fragrance. Flowers convert to seeds and pods. The twelve-inch pods fall from the trees in late autumn.

Red Beech, or Copper Beech: an umbrella-shaped tree growing up to sixty feet in height with a possible forty feet of width at the top. The dense red foliage absorbs almost all sunlight so very few plants, except lawn grass, will grow in its vicinity. An upland tree requiring dry soil it, like the Norway Maple, develops close limb structure to become very dense. Slow growing and long living, it is highly prized by those who admire its red color throughout the summer months.

Golden Chain: a twenty-foot-tall tree with strings of eight- to eighteen-inch lengths of yellow flowers in early spring. It has a strong leader, causing it to look pointed near the top. Diameter of top is eight to ten feet. It grows best in a medium moist soil.

Golden Rain: similar to the Golden Chain except that flowering time is mid-summer instead of mid-spring. Normal shape is a more round top with a height slightly taller than its cousin.

Flowering Peach: beautiful flowering trees with wide variation of blossoms that do not do well in cold climates of the northern United States. Flowering Peach is subject to the same insects and problems as the fruiting peach.

Paw-Paw: a small tree related to a family of tropical trees called the Custard Apple family. It grows banana-shaped fruits that can be eaten out of hand or cooked into desserts. The one-inch diameter blossom is purple. Both the common and the Dwarf Paw-Paw are upland trees. Another type grows best in wet soils and can grow up to sixty feet tall.

Sweetgum: a very large tree requiring medium wet soil. It is noted for many characteristics. The leaf is star-shaped, five to eight inches in size, and is pleasantly fragrant when crushed. The flower converts to long-stemmed hanging balls that dry in autumn, turn brown, then crack to release seeds. The name is due to wounds that permit sap to ooze out to form a thick jell that is chewed by some as a gum.

Ginkgo, or Maidenhair Tree: a fast growing upland tree with smooth greenish bark. It lines the streets of many towns and cities.

Its strong leader shoots upward to fifty feet. Diameter of branching at top is relatively narrow. An interesting tree for home driveways.

Mulberry: a family of three trees called the Paper, Red, and White, of which the Red is the most important. This upland tree, which grows as tall as thirty feet, is interesting both for leaf and fruit. Leaves are three to ten inches in length, and wood is reddish-brown with smooth ridges. Flowering takes place April through June. The fruit is half an inch in diameter by three quarters of an inch long; the berry-like fruits hang on slender stems from the branching. When ripe a slight jar to the branch will drop fruit to the ground. Some people collect the fruits by laying a plastic sheet beneath the tree and shaking it vigorously. Fruits are eaten as is or with cream and sugar. Their taste is pleasant. Another interesting tree to grow if it is placed in an out-of-the-way location.

Nature's trees: I have imposed the name on all those trees growing in the wild. Trees in their natural state usually have more imperfections than do those growing in nurseries because of competition. Nature corrects in her own way and at her own pace. In searching for trees in nature one should be selective. Avoid one-sided ones because they have been too close to another, avoid sharply crotched trees because such trees may split under stress as their size increases. Look for those that are likely to dig easily. The most serious error is made by taking trees at the wrong time of year and selecting too large a tree. Trees in the wild should be moved only when they are fully dormant. Deciduous trees can be moved after one or two frosts in autumn, or when all foliage has dropped. November and early December, late March and early April are ideal for such endeavors. Select deciduous trees no taller than eight to ten feet. Cut off six- to twelve-inch portions of the top branching to compensate for roots that need to be cut in the digging. Shake the soil free from the roots for easier carrying. Keep the roots moist by thrusting them into a plastic bag, or obtain trees on a rainy day when roots can be exposed to the air without danger of drying. And, most important of all, obtain the permission of land owners before going into private land to search for trees.

I have obtained hundreds of trees in this manner. They were subsequently planted in my nursery to grow larger and be sold at a later date. Some would be selected while still in leaf and marked so as to be identified when dormant. Most were selected during the gathering process. The types of trees selected were those that grew wild in my general area. Knowledge of which grew in high land and which in low land was helpful. The identification between Scarlet and Silver Maple was difficult, but not important, as both will be planted to be identified when in leaf the following spring. A homeowner might desire to be more precise. I am told there is a difference in the odor of broken wood between Scarlets and Silvers. The trunk wood of the Scarlet is a lighter shade of gray. Both have red twigs (the eight- to ten-inch length of newest wood in the branches) and both grow in the same moist soils. Sometimes, dropped leaves give a clue. Certainly, leaves still on the tree identify one or the other. In early spring Scarlet flowers with dangling red blossoms which positively identify it. Root systems are identical.

Sugar Maple is found more commonly than Norway. Sugar bark is tan colored while Norway is gray. Sugars shoot upward straight and tall with few branches. Norway is less straight, with branches already started closer to ground level, or with bulges in bark indicating bud growth underneath. The tips of Sugars are very sharply pointed, the Norway thick and blunt. The leaf of the Sugar is held to the wood directly while that of the Norway wraps itself halfway around the branch. When the leaves are alive and present, one torn loose will bleed a white mucous, the Norway being the only tree doing this.

Birch, like Maple, is sought in terrain suitable to the variety. Gray is by far the most common in moist soils, while Paper seeks higher land. Look for Birch as dark brown saplings with short white segment lines horizontal to the ground. Small birch, like maples, are generally in the area of parent trees, or in the direction that prevailing wind carry the seeds.

Aspen is a smooth greenish-white barked tree growing in upland soils. Avoid trees with dark imperfections in the bark on either the trunk or the branching. Aspen grows from extended roots of parent trees and from scattered seed.

Tuliptrees are usually on the prevailing wind side of parent trees. Look for tan bark with vertical strips, also enlarged buds. Parent trees are tall, straight, and have straw cups high up in the branching which remain year-round.

Red Leaf Maples do not grow in the wild. Some maples show bright red leaves in early spring but it is not a lasting red.

One time, experimentally, I dug five maples and five birch from the wild in late June. I removed all the foliage and planted all in good grade soil. All leafed out anew that same summer and continued to grow the following year. I forced the dormancy and each responded.

Do not be inhibited by this short listing of wild trees. Other varieties may grow in or near your surroundings.

Home Grown Fruits

In past years most families lived on farms. It was common practice to plant several kinds of fruits to supply the needs of the family, to sell to buyers for delivery to faraway cities, or to supply local canning factories. Change in living habits has reduced farm ownership to a coveted few, yet the desire to grow fruits is still with us. I hope the following explanation will aid those of you who plant fruit trees in your backyard.

A Mc'Intosh Apple tree with a heavily laden branch.

Row of Dwarf Apple trees, Empire variety, approximately ten-foot spacing.

This standard Northern Spy tree was planted in 1947. Note how the top has been removed. Note also the quantity of fruits. Limbs growing upward are cut off each year. This picture was taken in late September.

This sixty-year-old Mc'Intosh apple tree produces an average of twenty bushels per year. A bushel weighs fifty-six pounds.

Apples: A Complete Guide

There is a relationship between growing of nursery stock and growing fruit trees. Planting bare rooted trees is explained in previous discussion of trees so I will concentrate on the care of apples first, then move on to other fruits. Most of today's apple trees being planted are of the dwarf type. German horticulturists discovered a method to limit the root growth of trees, which in turn limits the size of the tree. Dwarfs can be Full Dwarf, Semi, or a size about half the size of a standard tree. The Dwarf, growing eight to ten feet, and the Semi-Dwarf, to fifteen feet, are generally preferable. Dwarfs were not available when I planted my orchard of standard trees, each planted forty feet from the other. Standard trees grow thirty feet high and thirty feet in diameter. Cutting the tops severely can restrict upper growth. I planted varieties to sell fruits on a roadside stand. I had planted a number of both Northern and Red Spy. The Red Spy were colorful, as well as large and tasty, but I cut the trees due to infestation of bitter rot. This hard-to-control disease causes freckle-like spots on the apple's surface that continues to penetrate deeper into the fruits when they are in storage. It is bitter to the taste, hence the name. Northerns are not as susceptible to the disease.

Apple trees develop fruit buds more prominently in early spring than leaf buds. Scan your tree before any buds open and you can make a reasonable estimate of the amount of blossom. Naturally a late frost can injure blossom, so blossoms don't always guarantee a crop. But a crop cannot come without the blossom.

My experience in pruning apples has only been on standard trees. I assume pruning dwarfs is similar with fewer cuttings removed. Fruit grown on dwarf trees is of the same size and quality as on standard trees. Different varieties grow different shapes. Spy, Delicious, Red Astrican, Mc'Intosh, and others grow upright with branching reaching outward. Twenty Ounce, Courtland and others grow in an umbrella shape. Pruning is a thinning out of branches, including the cutting off of branches that curve upward from the horizontal branches. It is also proper to remove limbs that grow downward so that remaining branching is on a flat plane to the extent possible. A correctly pruned tree will have layers, or tiers, of branching sufficiently apart from each other so sunlight can penetrate, so fruit is exposed for spraying, and so fruit-laden limbs will not lay atop one another to cause injury to fruit in strong wind. Each tree needs to be thought of as an individual and pruned accordingly. Pruning is generally done when trees are dormant in the months of January, February, and March. However it can be done without excessive harm at other times of year, if circumstances warrant it.

Apples can be classified according to the time of ripening. Early ripening apples are usually soft textured, bruise easily, do not store long after being picked, and generally drop from the tree more easily. They are referred to as summer apples. A few examples of summer apples are Lodi, Early Mc'Intosh, Dutchess, Red Astrican, and many others in addition to these four.

Autumn apples ripen in September. Fruit is more solid and storage time after picking considerably longer. Summer apples are usually wholesome for eating when freshly picked. Autumn apples improve in quality within a week or two after being picked. Autumn apples will store for up to two months in proper storage, and handling is not as great a problem. Autumn apples are Late Mac's, Twenty Ounce, Wealthy, Courtland, Empire, and also many others not listed here.

Winter apples are, as the name suggests, at their peak in cold weather. The fruit is generally very hard at the time of picking, will withstand more punishment without bruising while being handled, and needs to be in storage a considerable length of time to gain peak flavor. Obviously storage can be, as the name implies, the months of November through February. I am referring to home storing and not industrial storing. Winter apples are fewer in number—Northern Spy, Red Rome, Ida Red and, to some extent, Red and Yellow Delicious. Red Delicious stores differently than Yellow Delicious. The former will soften and lose flavor after a time, while Yellow will shrivel from moisture loss but still retain flavor. Some people feel flavor of the Yellow is enhanced after the shriveling. Proper storage for apples is a moist storage. A shower of water dashed on apples in storage on a weekly basis will give them a longer storage life. Do not wrap them in newspaper, bury them in sawdust, or use any covering that draws moisture out of the fruit. Apples need the air movement that is natural in storage bins to dispense gas released by the continuing ripening process. Commercial storage preserves apples for extended life by removing oxygen, which aids ripening, replacing it with an inert gas and lowering temperature. So, we have apples available all year long. A mild warning to homeowners: Because of acid content in most apples the fruits will not be destroyed unless the temperature lowers below approximately twenty-eight degrees Fahrenheit. A temperature of forty degrees is ideal for storage of apples while temperatures below that figure for sustained periods of time appear to lessen flavor.

Growing good apples is difficult but can be done if the grower follows a basic spray schedule. Farmers who grow huge quantities for wholesale cannot take chances and spray from ten to thirteen times per growing season, the number somewhat dependent on frequency of heavy rainfall. A home orchard need not be so precise. I grew up in a time when all trees were of the standard type. My knowledge is based on that type of tree. I assume dwarf varieties need similar care even though hand labor and spraying equipment are different. In my day spraying was done with a gun-type device that concentrated spray only on the tree to be sprayed. Today's blast blowers throw out a heavy mist that saturates everything in the orchard—tree, ground, birds nesting in trees. Spray contaminates ground water to eventually flow into ponds and lakes. It increases spray costs but decreases labor costs, a change made necessary to keep the price to the consumer competitive with apples from outside the United States. The home owner can rely on the old-fashioned method to care for his orchard. If upward reach is not high enough the user can use a stepladder or platform. When should I spray and with what mixture is the often asked question. I will answer that question.

It is a warm sunny day in late April, The weatherman, or woman, says no rain is expected for the next twenty-four hours and the temperature that night will hover above forty. A look at the apple tree tells you the buds are enlarging but not yet showing leaf or blossom emergence; but that time will come soon. It is time to put on the dormant spray, not an essential spray for that year's apple crop but to keep trees healthy for future crops. A dormant spray is with dormant oil, a special oil that is formulated to mix with water to form a milk-like mixture. It is harmless to human skin. It can be purchased from any garden store in pint, quart, or gallon containers. It is to be used only once per season, although commercial growers may use lesser quantities in successive sprays, so buy accordingly. The percentage of mixture to water is stated on the can. Using more than the stated amount will not injure the tree, nor will it do a better job. Roughly, the quantity is one cup of oil to four gallons of water. It is well to use a pesticide also at this time. Pesticide is a powder that dissolves in water. It kills insects by body contact and by poisoning leaf surfaces that may be eaten. Mix the two together in water and spray all surfaces of the tree, or trees—apple, cherry, peach, or whatever—being careful to wet the underside of the limbs as well as the upper sides. Crawling insects will die from contact, scale insects will be smothered under their protective shell and also die. The San Jose scale that attacks apple trees adheres to the bark surface to secrete a shell of material, similar to lime, that forms a kind of house. Underneath that protection the insect feeds on sap by boring into the cambium layer. Dormant oil is the one spray that will destroy this insect when it is not in the crawling stage. In the crawling stage it can be killed with ordinary pesticide, but that stage does not occur until much later in the summer.

The second spray is applied in what is called the pink cluster stage. This spray, and successive sprays, must contain both a pesticide and fungicide. In this instance the pesticide is to control the apple miner, an insect that lays eggs in leaf clusters, from which young hatch to do damage to foliage in August and September. This small white winged insect pierces the undersides of leaves to deposit eggs. The leaf injury causes a raised welt on the upper leaf surfaces while larva feed on chlorophyll which the tree badly needs at this time of fruit development. I should explain that the pink cluster stage is when blossoms are beginning to show color. The fungicide is to control scab, a plant growth that mars apple surfaces. Spores rise from maturing fungi on ground debris to attach to leaf surfaces. Some wash downward to adhere to apple surfaces, and multiply to form the skin lesion known as scab. A fungicide normally cannot destroy scab already present but it does place a coating on leaf surfaces to prevent more infection. Both pesticides and fungicides are adhesives but excessive rain will wash both away. The rule is if two inches of rain falls in a short span of time, spraying should be repeated.

The third spray is a mixture of the two, primarily to combat the plum curculio. This winged insect cuts a crescent-shaped groove in an apple's surface to lay a single egg. The reason for the groove is thought to prevent the growing apple from crushing the egg prior to its hatching. Once hatched the egg converts to a maggot, commonly referred to as a worm. This spray is a preventative one. Insects are wise. A mother will not place her eggs in a contaminated tree that could harm her young.

The fourth spray is to encourage the apple maggot fly to go elsewhere. Again it is preventative. The apple maggot is a problem from mid-June through July. This insects lays eggs under the skin of the fruit, eggs that hatch into miniature maggots that bore through the apple, leaving brown tunnels. Cut open an unsprayed apple and the brown streaks are very obvious. Cutting open an insect-free apple reveals a white, unmarked interior. The apple maggot can require approximately three sprays within that month-and-a-half period. If desired a seventh spray can be applied in August with pesticide only, as the scab infestation time is past. If scab is present it originated earlier in the growing season.

Different varieties of apple are continually being developed. In spite of this many of the older varieties continue to be in demand. All of the older types are available on dwarf trees. Most apples are self-pollinating, that is the male and female components grow on the same tree, but planting two or more types aids pollination. I suggest an early summer apple, an autumn one, and a third for winter. If a winter storage facility is lacking, apples can be converted into sauce to be preserved by canning. I am also informed that partly-cooked apple pieces and sauce can be frozen for future use. In my day preserving apples for pie the following summer meant drying them. They were peeled and cored, cut into three-eighths-inch slices, subjected to burning sulphur smoke to retain the whiteness, and dried by heat moving up through a slotted kiln. The result was rubbery dried fruit that was stored by placing it in cloth bags to hang from dry upstairs roof rafters. Tasty for chewing as a snack or, placed in clean water they would regain size lost by the drying to make a reasonably good tasting pie.

Apples must have qualities to endear themselves to the public. Opinions differ and tastes differ. Some are too tart for hand eating but make superb sauce and pie. Some need additives like sugar and cinnamon to enhance their flavor. In my opinion the best flavored apples are:

Red Astrican—pie and sauce
Twenty Ounce—eating from hand, pie, and sauce
Mc'Intosh—same as above
Red Delicious—eating from hand
Empire—eating from hand, pie, and sauce
Courtland—eating from hand, Waldorf salad
Wealthy—pie and sauce
Northern Spy—eating from hand, pie, and sauce
Matsu, or Chrispan—eating from hand, pie, and sauce

Each of these and others will be described in more detail in the following attempt to describe apples currently being grown in home orchards.

Lodi: a large (three and a half to four and a half inch) apple with very white flesh ripening in early August. The skin is green, changing to yellow when ripe. Interior is juicy and crisp when ripe but softens to decay in less than a week's time. Used for sauce and pie. Apples fall from tree when ripe.

Jerseymac: a Mc'Intosh cross that is relatively new. Has tart flavor, white flesh, red skin. Grows to a three- to four-inch diameter. Will store after picking for up to a month. Ripening in late August its use is for hand eating, pie, and sauce.

Tydeman: another late August apple with red skin that resembles Jerseymac in size and use. Storing time is approximately a month.

Wealthy: a red striped apple ripening in August. It is green while growing, and changes to yellow with bright red vertical stripes when ripe. Trees fruit heavily and apples drop easily when ripe. A tart apple for hand eating but good for pie and sauce. Ripening time is late August, keeping time about one month. Size is about three inches; the fruit is slightly longer than it is wide.

Red Astrican: an apple from the '30s that is relatively unknown in the '90s. Many, many apples have been discarded along the way—Baldwins, Wagners, Talisman Sweets, Maiden Blushes, Russets, Sheep Noses, and others but why the Red Astrican? Ripening in late July, it is ideal for sauce and pie, slightly tart for hand eating unless you prefer tartness. The green color changes to a bright red on the sun side first, coloring the entire apple when fully ripe. Trees are very productive; hand thinning or severe pruning of branching is recommended to prevent overloading of branches. Fruits are almost two and a half to four inches with white interiors. Like all early apples, fruit is at its peak for a limited period of about two weeks. In dark cool storage, keeping time can be up to two months. Apples do not ripen at the same time so picking must be selectively done over a two- to three-week period, which may be one reason it is no longer planted.

Mc'Intosh: Mc'Intosh comes in an early and late variety. I was disappointed in the early type because of its smaller size, but the quality was similar. I will discuss the late. This juicy, white-fleshed apple ripens in mid-September. Trees are very productive and need severe pruning to prevent branch breakage from overloading. Fruits average about three and a half inches in diameter, are red skinned in full sunlight and half-red/half-green in shade. Ripe fruit drops easily. Fruit bruises easily and care must be taken in handling. Storage life is about three months in good home storage. The time to pick is when the undersides turn pale yellow for those in shade and, of course, those fully red. Macs make a flavorful but juicy pie and a rather juicy sauce. Mixed with a drier variety of apple they add both moisture and flavor. Mc'Intosh was first introduced about 1878.

Twenty Ounce: a larger than usual apple that has been around a long time. It ripens in mid-September. The name implies its individual weight, but most range about half that amount. Apple trees grow differently and apples on trees grow differently. Twenty Ounce grow on trees that are umbrella-shaped. The slender end branches don't appear to be strong enough to support large fruits but none break. The fruits hang as if tied by string, requiring a tug to remove them at harvest time. Grassy green in the growing stage, the fruits slowly turn a light yellow and develop red streaking on the sunlight side. The flesh is an off-white, mealy in texture, relatively dry, but has excellent flavor. Twenty Ounce is good for hand eating, great in sauce and pie. Ripening in mid-September, the storage time is about two months with no apparent decline in cooking quality.

Courtland: a medium to large red apple with white flesh that is similar in storage quality to Mc'Intosh. A good flavored apple for hand eating as well as the making of pie and sauce. It has the added distinction of flesh that retains its white color for a considerable time and thus is often used in salads. Trees grow umbrella-style in much the same manner as Twenty Ounce. Pruning needs to be severe to prevent overloading.

Empire: one of the best varieties of modern apples. This apple, of a four-inch diameter, is picked in late October. At that time it will develop a deep purple color. It is resistant to scab, so needs fewer sprays. It is excellent for hand eating, for pie and sauce. It stores well, up to and past the holiday season of Christmas. It is supposed to be another cross with Mc'Intosh but lacks the Mac's tendency to bruise easily. I recommend it highly.

Red Delicious: an all-red apple with a sweet flavor. The shape is slightly longer than wide, the greatest diameter at the top. When fruits first form they turn upward like miniature candles but weight forces them downward one hundred eighty degrees at harvest time. Trees are very productive, usually growing full crop yearly. Branches tend to reach out horizontal to the ground. Fruits hang on the tree well into autumn to become a deep purple. Common Red averages about three and a half inches in diameter but an improved variety called Double Red will attain close to a five-inch diameter. Storage is two to three months with flesh softening after that to become mushy. Use is primarily eating out of hand.

Yellow Delicious, sometimes called Golden Delicious; a yellow apple, more round than the Red but approximately the same size. Fruits are more solid than Reds, the flesh is whiter, the storage time longer. Yellows appear to shrivel more than Reds if left in storage too long but normal crisp interior remains crisp and tasty. Trees are more umbrella shaped than Reds. Fruit does not drop easily. Color is solid bright yellow with brown freckles. Use is eating out of hand.

Northern Spy: an old-fashioned apple of large size that is prized as a winter apple. Fruits are very solid, heavy, and their keeping quality excellent. Color is yellowish with dull red cheeks, sometimes streaked with vertical red lines. Flesh is off-white, juicy, with a tang unlike any other apple. Use is hand eating, pie, and sauce. Trees are the wide spreading type, requiring severe pruning yearly. Spies have two characteristics that cause a second thought about this variety in a home orchard. They live a long life so do not begin to bear fruit on standard trees until planted up to twelve years. Trees bear fruits every second year with scant fruit in the off year. This may not be true of dwarf trees. Fruits are late in the picking, just prior to cold weather in November. All fruits do not ripen at the same time so fruits must be selectively picked. Quality improves in storage, continuing well into spring. Being a late ripening apple, blossoming time is also late and thus not subject to late spring frosts as are other varieties.

Rome, sometimes called Rome Beauty: a shiny red, hard, winter apple that stores well. It does not have sufficient flavor to create demand so is not a popular fruit.

Ida-Red: a beautiful red apple of large size that ripens late in October, keeps very well in storage, and has a distinctive flavor that is unappealing to many. Not a popular apple for home growing.

Macoun: an old type apple with good flavor. Skin is dark red, size on the small side, keeping quality very good.

Matsu, or Chrispan: a Japanese apple that is new. It is large, exciting, with good flavor. Great for eating, pie, and sauce. The color is a dull brownish-green overall. Being a late ripening apple, storage life is long. I recommend growing this Chrispan fruit.

Being an old-timer, I have seen the coming and going of many varieties of apples. Some very good ones have been abandoned for reasons unknown. I will list a few.

Baldwin: a hard red winter apple.

Russett: a brownish-skinned apple noted for making good cider.

Wagner: a white-with-red-cheeks apple with tasty white flesh.

Sheep Nose: an oblong shaped red apple with pleasant taste.

Ben Davis: a beautiful shiny red apple without flavor.

Maiden Blush: a yellow apple with bright red cheeks.

Bottle Greening: a green apple growing to eight inches in diameter.

Hubbord: a dry apple with good flavor that stores well.

Pound Sweet: a juicy summer apple of large size with good flavor.

Talman Sweet: a small yellow sweet apple used mainly by being cooked in a sugary syrup.

The four described more completely—Twenty Ounce, Ida-Red, Red Astrican, and Northern Spy—are old-time varieties that have survived the passage of time.

Apples have non-lethal diseases that can occur from time to time. One is fire blight, a show of dead end branches in late July that resemble wood burnt by fire. The blackened wood, due to infection and dry brown leaves, needs to be severed below the infection. The cut branches are burned or buried under one to two inches of earth. The infection can be severe one year, less severe the next. If branches are not removed trees will recover.

Mildew can also be a sporadic visitor. This parasitic plant is generally widespread before the human eye is aware of it. It is prevalent in hot dry weather to change the dark green of healthy foliage to a gray appearance. It affects fruit quality but will not kill a tree. Too late for preventative control it is combated by the use of powdered sulphur in the amount stated on the package. Do not use more than the stated amount as sulphur can harm foliage also if used carelessly.

Aphids are a continual annoyance to apple growers. These mite-like insects can multiply rapidly on the undersides of leaves, curling the leaf by sucking its juices and thus making it difficult to control with the normally used pesticides. Spraying more frequently is the answer if aphids become a problem. Aphids cause deformed fruits by utilizing chemicals provided by the tree for apple development.

Two kinds of mice can also become problems. One gnaws at the trees' outer bark, including the cambium layer, particularly during winter when food is scarce. Prevention involves using poisoned grain placed in an accessible-to-mice crib that prevents harm to birds and other animals plus encircling the trunks of the trees with screen from tight ground level to about a twenty-four-inch height. A second variety of mouse lives under ground to destroy trees by eating their root surfaces. Control is most difficult as the mice rarely emerge into the open. Sometimes a tree root area can be saturated by sufficient water to fill all underground cavities and thus drown these mischief-makers. Using this kind of water saturation one time will not harm the tree.

Mature fifteen-year-old Sweet Cherry, Emperor Francis Variety.

Eight-year-old Sour Cherry tree, Montmorency Variety.

Sweet Cherry

The usual times of year for planting Sweet Cherry are late in autumn and early in spring. The tree size for planting is five to six feet. Saplings are normally straight trunked, dark colored wood, bare rooted, and with some top branching. Sweets require a rich, well-drained soil. Some varieties of Sweet Cherry can be purchased in a dwarf size but I will describe only standard sized trees. Sweet Cherry grows to a twenty-five- to thirty-foot height with a spread of branching almost as great. It is a tree with a life span of fifty years or more and consequently does not begin to produce fruit until several years after being planted. Once the fruiting starts, trees continue to bear yearly unless blossom is injured by unusually late frost. A Sweet Cherry is not self pollinating so a second variety must be with in bee travelling distance for best pollination. Bees usually travel less than 500 feet from nest or from hive. Some wild cherries, if growing nearby, can act as pollinators. Pruning of Sweet Cherry consists of removal of suckers, and occasionally one or two branches to lessen density. Wounds are left to air dry and heal by themselves.

Most Sweet Cherries ripen on or close to the Fourth of July. The health of the tree determines the quality of fruit produced. Healthy trees have long slender leaves with a dark green color. Yellowing of foliage prior to or after harvest is indication of fungus. Foliage needs one dormant spray prior to emergence of leaves, a second spray with fungicide just prior to blossoming. It is most important to apply another fungicide spray just as small cherries are beginning to shed the fruiting shuck. This spray will control brown rot. Brown rot is exactly what it is called; the cherries turn brown and fall from the tree. A fourth spray of fungicide can be applied prior to harvest if foilage indicates a need, and one or two can follow harvest for a similar reason. Ferbam, a fungicide, is used by commercial growers but garden stores supply other brands of fungicides that also do the job. Add a pesticide to the brown rot control spray to deter insects that may be inclined to pierce fruits to deposit eggs.

Sweet cherries enlarge quickly, ripen quickly, and rot just as quickly. Picked cherries, even with stems still attached, will last only a short time, perhaps three to four days. Unpicked cherries will grow larger and sweeter but eventually will rot on the tree. Most need picking selectively as all do not ripen at the same time. Varieties of some sweet cherries are as follows:

Black Tartarian: a large, very sweet-tasting black cherry that is excellent for eating fresh. It is pollinated by either Emperor Francis or Napoleon.

Bing: another large black cherry used for the same purposes as is the Black Tartarian. It is pollinated by the Emperor or Napoleon.

Windsor: an almost black cherry with firm flesh that ripens in mid-July. It is pollinated by Emperor, Napoleon, and Royal Ann.

Hedlefinger, Lambert, and Lyons: also black cherries that are pollinated by Emperor, Napoleon, and Royal Ann.

Emperor Francis: a white cherry with red cheeks, about three-quarters of an inch in diameter, ripening in early July. It is pollinated by any one of the black varieties.

Napoleon and Royal Ann: two varieties similar to Emperor Francis, except Royal Ann is lighter in color and inclined to be cling stone. Cling stone indicates a difficult separation of pit from flesh.

Eating by birds, and other abuse, is always a problem to sweet cherry growers. The black varieties are always more susceptible, as black cherries turn to a bright red before turning to black. Birds are attracted by the red color. Netting can be purchased from most garden stores to protect fruit. Aluminum plates suspended in twine only deter birds for a short time. Commercial growers sometimes use a deterrent spray but most allow the birds their fill and salvage the remainder.

Sour Cherry

Sour Cherry comes in only two varieties, Early Richmond and Montmorency. The former is generally not planted because it bears small-sized fruits with larger pits. Richmond ripens fully two weeks prior to Montmorency and for a time was planted so as to extend the picking season. I believe that policy has been abandoned.

Montmorency is a dark red, sour-sweet, juicy cherry. Trees grow twelve to fifteen feet high with a rounded shape of top branching. Trees begin to bear fruit about the fifth year, first a scattering on the more central branching, then in succeeding seasons on outer branching also. Trees bear yearly unless blossoms are injured by late frost. A life span of about twenty years is to be expected, the best producing years from age five to twelve and a decline in production from then on. Sours are self-pollinating with spacing of trees at an orchard at about fifteen feet. Care consists of spraying at necessary intervals, an application of nitrate fertilizer in early spring, some pruning to thin branching, and the picking chore. Commercial growers use shakers to dislodge cherries from trees but hand picking is still done by many small orchard farmers. Unlike apples, which are tested for degree of softness in the interior to determine time for harvest, cherries are tested by eye for color and by crushing to determine sugar content. Unlike Sweets, Sour Cherries will hang on the tree to become darker in color, larger in size, and more sugary. Also fully ripe sours separate from the stems more easily. Used primarily in pie, fruits are also used in ice cream, desserts, and other ways.

Methods to preserve are canning, freezing, making into wine. Juice can also be boiled to make an unintoxicating beverage.

Sours need a rich, well-drained soil. Preventative sprays with pesticide and fungicide are used to control the fruit fly, an insect that pierces the cherry's skin to lay an egg which hatches into a maggot. Spray with the fungicide after fruits are picked, with a pesticide at weekly intervals starting when fruits are pea-sized. Sprays usually number either three or four.

Elberta Peach Tree.

Bartlett Pear Tree.

Peaches

Peaches are one of the most natural fruits that grow. Plant a pit and you have a fifty-fifty chance of growing a tree with edible peaches. The pit must go through a dormant period. Bury it in moist sawdust, peat, or sand, in a cellar or basement throughout the winter. When danger of freezing is over the following spring, remove it, crack open the shell, then plant the inner seed to a three or four inch depth. In about three weeks a growing tree will break the surface and in approximately three years it will begin to produce peaches. The fun part is that it may produce a superior peach to any you have ever eaten.

Peaches, like grapes, grow only on new wood. Peach trees need extensive pruning since new growth is usually vigorous. It is best to prune in late spring to prevent easily spread diseases and prevent winter injury to the wounds. Pruning can be done while trees are in blossom if care is taken not to injure fruit-producing wood that will remain on the tree.

Peaches are subject to harm by insects, by cankor, and by leaf curl. The first can be controlled by a dormant oil spray in early spring before buds begin to enlarge. This spray also helps control peach curl. Peach curl, the name given to an airborne disease that causes crinkling and discoloration of the leaf surface, is also controlled by fungicide spraying in late autumn, after the harvest has been removed. Normal insects are controlled by a mixture of pesticide-fungicide spray at the pink stage of blossoming, when the fruits are half an inch in size, one inch in size, with a fourth spray about July 15. The fungicide often used by commercial growers is Ferbam. If that is not obtainable other brands will suffice. Among the insects not fully controlled by sprays are borers. When spraying, particularly during the period of June 15 to August 1, wet the trunk and wood of the lower branches. If borer holes are discovered, probe within using small sized wire to pierce the borer. Also keep a thirty-six inch circle around the trunk free of grass and weeds. Cankor is another airborne disease that attacks bark. Indication is dark, wart-like, patches on an otherwise clear bark surface. If the patches are small, remove them by cutting with a draw-shave, or sharp knife. Sterilize the wound and the cutting tool with a mixture of chlorine and water, or with alcohol.

Peach lovers must keep in mind that peach is a southern tree. Many good varieties will not survive northern winters. Among the ones that will survive and have proven themselves over the years are Golden Jubilee, Rochester, Red Haven, Hale Haven, and Elberta. All are free-stone peaches, all are good for eating out of hand, for canning, or for freezing. I am informed that a preservative, which can be purchased at grocery stores, is necessary to prevent discoloration of fruit that is intended for the freezer. Descriptions of the five varieties follow.

Golden Jubilee: a rather small, perhaps two-inch-diameter round peach, very juicy, very sweet with excellent flavor. Ripens in early August. Trees bear every year. Soil needs to be relatively dry.

Rochester: a medium-sized peach with a red cheek. Very good flavor.

Red Haven: a small to medium peach with red skin and red flesh. Flavor is excellent.

Hale Haven: a large round peach with grayish-yellow skin. Flavor is good. This peach needs a second variety for pollination.

Elberta: a late peach ripening in late September. Fruits are large, oblong in shape, are yellow skinned with a red to pink side. Since the Rochester, Red Haven and Hale Haven ripen in mid-September the Elberta is the last locally grown peach to be harvested.

Pears

Pears are one of the easier fruits to grow. Damage to foliage by insects is minimal. Pruning is more simple, consisting of removal of suckers, those fast-growing shoots that grow seasonally from structural wood. They indicate that a tree is healthy and vigorous, yet if permitted to grow would convert the tree's energy into foliage instead of fruit. Pruning of pears is done in winter, as with apples, and only occasionally does a branch other than a sucker have to be removed. Pears are upright trees with branching growing almost vertically. Planting distance is about twelve feet. Soil requirement is, as for all fruits, good grade and well drained.

Most pears are not self-pollinating and need a second variety. Pear trees begin to produce a few fruits several years after being planted, and bearing is alternately light and heavy from that time on. Excessive rainfall when trees are blossoming, or too cold a temperature for pollinating insect movement, can cause scant crops. Two diseases also affect pears. One is fire blight. This airborne disease is a fungus that destroys the end tips of branches. Indication is dying of end tips in otherwise healthy-looking trees. Remove it by cutting off several inches into the living wood and destroy by burning or burying underground. This is not a common disease. The second, more common, disease is pear psylla, a mite-like insect that sucks juice from structural wood. Indication is a soot-like dusting on branches. Control is by application of a dormant oil spray prior to leaf emergence and several sprays with pesticide during the growing season.

A fungicide needs to be added to the pesticide to curtail any scab or mildew that may be present.

I will attempt to describe the Bartlett, both red and green, Bosc, Seckel, Clapp's Favorite, and Shelby. Additional pears that I will not describe are Maxine, Moonglow, Sure Crop, Starkcrimson, Comice, Magness, Fame, Dutchess, and Reimer Red. All of the latter are unknown varieties to me.

The Green Bartlett is the pear commonly grown by commercial orchard owners for sale to canneries. It is an ideal tree for home orchards as well. The pear ripens around September 1. It is picked, like most pears, while in the green hard state and placed in darkened storage to ripen further. Ripe pears take on a yellow skin, the texture softens and becomes more juicy, the aroma seeps outward to fill the surrounding air. Bartletts are tapering fruits, about three to three and a half inches in diameter at the base, with dark green smooth skin. Ripe interiors are moderately moist, and have good flavor. Keeping time after ripening is approximately one week. Place in the refrigerator for longer keeping. Bartlett needs the Keiffer or Seckel for pollination. Trees must be closer than 500 feet for mutual visiting by bees. Note: The only reason for growing Keiffer is for pollination purposes. Its fruit is of no value.

Red Barlett is a red-skinned pear that ripens about September 20. It is smaller than the Green with a stronger pear flavor. Being a late pear means keeping time is longer, possibly two to three weeks from harvest. Pollination is by Keiffer or Seckel.

Clapp's Favorite is larger than Bartlett, with a sweet juicy interior. Skin is light green, ripening time about September 1, keeping quality about one week after being picked. Pollination is by Keiffer or Seckel.

Shelby is another large juicy pear, excellent for eating from hand. Ripening in early September, it has a shelf life of about one week. Pollination is by Keiffer or Seckel.

Bosc is a late pear, ripening in late September. It is slightly larger than Bartlett, has a russet-colored skin, good flavor and rather dry interior. It keeps several weeks after harvest. Pollinator is Keiffer or Seckel.

Seckel is a small, perhaps one inch in diameter, pear that ripens in mid-September. Trees may grow very tall, up to forty feet, and slender. Pollination is by Bartlett, Bosc, Clapp's Favorite, and others. Use is making pickled pears. Fruits are studded with cloves and boiled in a sugary syrup, to be eaten when cooled, or canned for future use.

Plums and Prunes

Prunes belong to the family of plums. They differ greatly in texture. Plums originated in Japan while prunes came from a European source. Prunes are self-pollinating but plums need a second variety. Prunes grow on upright trees while plums usually grow ten to twelve feet in height with a top spread roughly the same size. Both need to be sprayed with both fungicide and pesticide. The fungicide must be applied prior to blossom and after fruits are harvested, to control black knot and brown rot. The former attacks structural wood to cause rough blisters with secretion of fluids. If possible cut the affected area away from healthy wood and sterilize the wound by applying a coating of household chlorine bleach mixed with water. Burn or bury the debris. Application of a fungicide mixture during developing of fruits is to control brown rot, a disease that causes immature fruits to turn brown and drop from the tree. Pesticide spraying when fruits are pencil size and at ten-day intervals are preventative measures against the plum curculio. This insect lays a single egg in growing fruit that hatches into what most refer to as a worm.

Varieties of Plums are Beauty, Shire, Abundance, Burbank, and Santa Rosa. There may be others in addition to these named. Prunes are Stanley and Fellenberg, the latter being the larger in size. Both are excellent quality. Fungicides and pesticides are available at most garden supply stores. Both are mixed with water in the proper amounts to do the job required.

Both plums and prunes are at their peak when fully ripe. Prunes turn from green to red to blue, continuing on to dark blue. At the later stage they separate from the stem very easily. Storage life after picking can be as long as two weeks. Uses are eating fresh, canning, and making prune preserves. Some types can be dried for snack eating. Perhaps there are other uses as well as those mentioned.

Nut Trees

Black Walnut, Hickory, and Butter are northern nut trees. The shell is very hard. The Pecan, Hazelnut, Filbert, Chestnut, and English Walnut are all warm climate trees. Varieties of each have been developed that withstand colder temperatures without injury and, consequently, attempts are made to grow these varieties more and more northward. All goes well unless the temperature lowers to an unusual level. If it does the protection surrounding the trees becomes a factor as to whether they live or die.

Black Walnut is a very hardy tree, growing to sixty feet tall with about the same footage in top diameter. The wood is dark, very hard, very highly prized in the manufacture of furniture. Black is an upland tree, slow growing, exterior bark rough, the leaf compound with six pairs of leaflets opposite each other on the common stem. The sap is of strong odor, light colored until exposed to air, then turning to a dark brown shade that resists removal by common soap and water. The blossom is a grape-like cluster of whitish flowers that result in clusters of up to four nuts. Nuts are encased in a thick green shell that enlarges to two inches and falls from the tree when frosted. Newly dropped nuts can be removed from shells by smashing the shell with a hammer, running over it with heavy equipment, placing a quantity in a strong enclosure and slicing away the shells with a square-lipped shovel. The exposed nuts must be stored for a few weeks to dry to become tasty. Actually they will store indefinitely. When dry a sharp blow by a hammer on the narrow side of the nut will split the shell so as to allow the meat to be removed.

Empty walnut shells can be sliced with a hand saw to make bracelets, the segments held together by elastic bands threaded through holes drilled in the outer rim of the shell segment. Black is subject to only the web worm as an injurious insect. However it does have one disadvantage: it seeps a toxin into the soil by the root system, so, to my knowledge, nothing else will grow in the vicinity except lawn grass.

Butter Nut

Butter Nut grows slightly smaller than does the Black Walnut. It does not contaminate the growing area. The nut is more oblong, with a thin covering. Removing the covering is easier after the husk has dried; a few taps with a hammer will pulverize it to expose the inner shell. Butter Nuts need to be set on end on a solid foundation and hit sharply with a hammer on one end to break the shell. Neither Black Walnut nor Butter Nut surrender meats easily. The flavor of the Butter Nut is sweet and mild, in contrast to the pungent aroma and flavor of the Black Walnut. Attacking insects are few. Leaves are compound. Trees are upland type trees.

Hickory Nut

Hickory Nut grows both in cultivation and in the wild. The tall tree is easily identified by narrow bark slabs that break loose at the bottom to curve outward from the trunk but remain attached at the top. Wild Hickory Nuts can be either sweet or bitter. Both are encased in thin shells that separate easily to the cream-colored nut. Nuts should be set on their narrow side and given a sharp blow with a hammer to free the meats. The meats are tasty. Hickory trees are straight and tall, with lower branches dying and dropping as the tree ages. The wood is very strong, used in the making of shovel handles and handles for other hand held tools. Trees are upland trees and require well-drained soil. Like other nuts, the meats have to dry for a time for best taste. When dry, nuts will store indefinitely.

English Walnut

English Walnut are southern trees. The Carpathian is a variety that grows more northward than most but it, too, dies when temperatures fall below normal winter temperatures. This type, an upland tree growing to about thirty feet in height, needs a second variety for pollination. English Walnut grows slowly, and will bear nuts every second year after reaching maturity. Mature trees begin to produce at about ten years, a scattering of nuts at first with increased amounts from age fifteen on. The trees have a long lifespan. The nuts have a slightly thicker shell than southern varieties but the flavors of the meats are similar.

Scion branch as cut from tree. Prepared scion with leaves removed and butt end tapered.

A successful graft, done in June and photographed in August.

*A segment of end branch prepared to receive scion.
Note screwdriver position.*

*Four years after being grafted, a tree producing both
Red and Yellow Delicious apples.*

The Arts of Budding and Grafting

Apple trees grow from apple seeds. I have not tried to grow trees from seed but wild trees are commonly discovered so I am assuming they are growing from seeds. Most seeds need to be removed from the pulp, air dried for a time, then stored in damp peat moss or sand. Normally they are removed in early spring and planted. Peach seeds need the hard shell broken to release the inner seed. Perhaps apple seeds need to be opened also. Budding is the method of converting a wild seedling to a desired variety. The wild tree is permitted to grow to finger thickness size. Close to the base, just above ground level, a bud is inserted. The time for insertion is when the tree is vigorously growing, usually in late May and early June. First, let me explain the composition of the bud to be inserted.

Beneath the bark of every living tree is a green layer called the cambium layer. It is the lifeline of the tree. Destroy it and the tree dies. Like a wound on a human hand it will heal injury to itself. A bud is the beginning of a swelling in the bark that eventually will grow into a branch. Both are needed. A cut in the parent tree is made to secure a segment of the cambium layer on the one side and a bud on the opposite side. A figure tee cut is made to expose the cambium layer in the tree to be budded. The flaps are pried open, the bud inserted with the bud facing an upright stance, the flaps released and all tightly bound with a special tape called grafting tape. The wound is made watertight with grafting wax, which is applied by finger pressure. The bud, if it takes, will begin to grow. When it grows sufficiently tall the wild growth will be severed. The tree will now produce the same fruit as the tree from which the bud was taken. Almost every shrub and tree that you may purchase was developed through the budding process.

Budding is the process for converting the entire tree to a common fruit. Grafting is a process to convert a part of a tree to a different variety while the untouched branching continues to produce the same fruit as previously. Thus a segment of a wild apple tree producing fruit of little or no value can be made to grow Mac's, Twenty Ounce, or any other desired choice of apple. Some nurseries like to advertise "5-n-1" apple trees. It is true that there are five varieties grafted onto one tree, but customers soon discover that varieties don't grow at the same rate and unless the fast-growing ones are severely pruned they soon take over the entire tree. If one desires more than one variety on a single tree it is well to limit those varieties to those that grow at similar rates per season. Grafting and budding are not restricted to apples. Pears can be grafted to other pear trees, peaches to peach trees, cherries to cherry trees, French lilacs to common purple lilac. The list is endless and satisfaction at gaining growth is great. One must keep in mind that trees comprise families and only those in a given family can be budded or grafted to the other. A pear cannot be grafted on an apple nor can an apple onto a pear. But apples can be grafted onto any type of apple tree including Crabapple.

Buds are used in budding, scions in grafting. Scions are usually the end branches of new growing stems. Lengths vary but three- to four-inch lengths are common. The leaf structure is removed to lessen drain on sap entry into the transplanted scion. The end bud is left intact. The cut end is tapered by cutting with a sharp knife. Keep the cuts parallel and flat, tapering both to a chisel shape. The branch to be prepared for receiving the graft is cut off cleanly. The thickness of the branch is not important, but one-inch thickness is ideal. Use the sharp knife again, using a hammering tool, to split the cut end dead center to a one-inch depth. Do not split more than necessary. Remove the knife, and drive a screwdriver into mid-center to force open the split. The scions, usually two, are inserted on either side so the edges of scions line up with the outer face of the branch. This lines up the cambium layers to facilitate the movement of nourishment. Grafting tape is ideal, but common plastic electrical tape can be used also, to wrap around the cut end after the screwdriver is removed to tighten the bond between scion and branch. I wrap two turns around the stub, stretching the plastic as I do so to increase the bonding pressure, then wrap the tape between the scions so as to seal off the end of the stub. Two wrappings in this way with another encircling each scion will ensure that outside moisture will remain outside. If successful, the scions will continue to look healthy and growth can be expected in about a month's time. The growth from an early spring graft can reach a length of three feet the first season. During the second year it will further grow to produce fruiting buds and further heal the point of graft. Fruits can be expected the third year.

Grafting is usually done the same time of season as is budding. My experiments in grafting in mid-summer showed that heat dried the scions rapidly, causing them to fail. I overcame this by coating the exteriors of the scions with moisture-retaining material. My first coatings were of white petroleum jelly. I was careful to coat all of the scion except the end bud. I continued grafting through July and August successfully. Some scions I coated with grafting wax. I am certain other types of coatings would be successful also. Do not expect 100 percent success at first attempt. Fifty percent success is average, up to ninety percent a great accomplishment. Keep in mind that late-summer graftings do not produce the amount of growth as early spring ones do.

I offer one caution. The cambium layer is a lifeline between root and branching. It must have sufficient branching to keep it active. Do not cut all the branches from a tree in grafting onto it a different fruit. Graft only a strategic number of branches in a given season. Allow existing branches to continue growing until grafted varieties are sufficiently large enough to sustain that lifeline. It may require three seasons to fully convert a medium-sized tree.

Converting a tree to a different fruit is most successful in late summer by cutting off branching earlier to force new growth. This growth, called suckering, is cut within inches of the supporting branch and grafted with a one-bud scion. Graft the tree at strategic intervals.

A fence-type arbor for supporting grapes.

A more artistic type of arbor.

Grapes

It seems proper to talk about growing grapes toward the end of this book because grapes are one of the last fruits to ripen fully, just prior to the onset of cold weather. Some claim that a frost is needed to put the sweet flavor into grapes but, in my opinion, that is error. What is needed for development of the ideal grape is the proper amount of three things—sunlight, water, and temperature. Naturally, a healthy vine in good textured soil is also important. Supporting this opinion is the statement often given by wine makers that this or that year produces excellent wine grapes. Evidently the more sugar in the grape the more potent the wine.

Grape varieties are usually the result of a process called layering. Using the tendency of grapes to root from any section of the vine that contacts the earth, a shallow excavation is dug so a portion of vine can be, literally, buried beneath the soil to remain one growing season. Sufficient roots will have developed so that segment can be cut free from the mother vine. It can be dug to be replanted and will produce the same type of grape as the vine from which it was taken.

Grapes grow best in a rich, well-drained soil. The life span is a long one, perhaps up to 100 years. Most need the support of a trellis, or fence, or overhead support of one sort or another. The tentacles will reach out to grasp solid objects and hold on but human assistance in the form of cloth or twine ties is needed to secure vines, especially in windswept areas. Supports made of wood are best. Do not make use of iron pipe as the iron becomes too hot in sunlight.

A heavy smooth wire commonly called grape wire number nine is often used to criss-cross wooden posts for overhead support.

Grapes need severe pruning to produce fruits. Commercial growers cut all wood off established vines to leave only a three- to five-foot trunk. The object is to produce large bunches. The fewer bunches a vine grows the larger each bunch, within reason.

When purchasing a grape vine to be planted do not prune the top as it is too late in the season. Dig a trenchlike hole not more than six inches deep to accommodate the root. The vine can be left to grow without support for one or two seasons. Then begin the pruning process and use of support for the vine. New vines can be classified as one, two, three, or four years old. Two- to three-year-olds are ideal for planting. A homeowner can permit vines to go up to twenty feet in length. If the vine is growing well the longer vine will grow bunches suitably large and in greater quantity. Pruning is done in the months of January, February, and March. Do not cut vines at any other time of year. To prune, start at the base of the vine and cut off all branching leaving stubs with one to two buds. The buds are prominent and each will grow a length of new vine with its clusters of bunches. Grapes are generally planted at ten feet distance so, when pruning, ends can be cut at about that length.

I have grown the following grapes: Concord, Seedless Concord, Niagara White, Fredonia, Delaware, and Catawba. In my opinion, unless you intend to grow varieties for wine making, grow only two, Blue Concord and White Niagara. Concord is for pie, sauce, wine, and other uses while Niagara is primarily a hand eating grape. Both are delicious. As grapes ripen fully the sweet odor of ripening is given off. It attracts bees that pierce the grape skin, so be aware in picking. Raccoons are attracted by the sweeter Niagara. They need to be trapped and transported elsewhere, unless state law prevents it.

Modern-day growing of grapes require spraying. A first spray of pesticide and fungicide is applied when buds first start to enlarge, and second just prior to blossoming. Blossoming produces spikes that extend out from the stem with tiny flowers at the end. A most important spray is when the blossom is ninety percent complete. This spray controls what is known as brown rot, a disease that afflicts grapes in the ripening stage. A fourth and fifth spray should be applied at ten-day intervals. Insects to be controlled are berry moth, curcilio, flea beetle, mealy bug, brown rot, and leaf-sucking insects such as Japanese beetle. Gathering up and burning discarded leaves in autumn assists in prevention of diseases.

Additional varieties of grape are: Caso, a red grape; Steuben, a light blue; and Golden Musket, a yellow. Also there are Buffalo and Van Buren, very dark colored and sweet, Concord and Interlaken, both seedless and large, and Romulus and Sheridan, other blue varieties.

Should I Buy Balled and Burlapped Trees or Bare Root Trees?

Nurseries generally purchase small trees that are dug by the grower with soil shaken from the roots. Such trees are said to be bare rooted trees. Most retail customers buy trees that are balled and burlapped, but occasionally have the opportunity to purchase bare rooted stock. This is particularly true when buying fruit trees from stores that do not, ordinarily, sell trees except in springtime. The reason for bare rooted stock is convenience.

Plant nurseries are often remote from populated areas. While, admittedly, balled and burlapped trees are superior to bare rooted trees, the cost of transportation for trees with roots encased in a ball of earth would make retail costs so great as to prohibit sales. A single balled and burlapped tree shipped a thousand miles would cost more to transplant than fifty similarly sized trees with bare roots. Retail nurseries buy trees bare rooted, plant the trees for a time until roots develop into the new soil, and then dig and sell the trees as balled and burlapped. Some nurseries plant bare rooted trees in containers of metal, plastic, or wood, to be grown in such containers and sold to customers to place on the customer the responsibility of transferring the container-grown plant to the ground. Some nurseries purchase balling machines in which the bare rooted trees are hydraulically balled and burlapped to give the impression of being nursery grown. The latter are generally round shaped balls whose only redeeming feature is roots that are kept moist by being encased in, hopefully, moist soil. Exposed roots are very delicate; they cannot be exposed to drying air to any degree without serious damage to the tree or shrub. Bare rooted trees shipped to nurseries have roots wrapped in quantities of moisture-laden moss. The whole is enclosed in plastic for further protection. The plastic-enclosed plants are shipped in heavy cardboard boxes for additional safeguarding. How the receiver handles that stock upon removal from the wrappings is very important to him and possible to the one who eventually purchases it.

Trees are not hardy solely because of variety. Southern states are the source of many, many trees because of lower labor costs, because some states contain large areas of land remote from population centers, and because of longer growing season. But the longer season also has disadvantages when sales are to the north. Trees do not have within themselves the hardiness to withstand cold temperatures. Silver Maples grow in all sections of New York State, but trees growing in Tennessee transported to New York in autumn and planted will not survive the winter. The same trees placed in protective storage to be planted in late spring will grow that summer and continue to grow in succeeding seasons. Apparently tolerance to low temperatures develops during that first summer season. This advice may not apply to many but I offer it regardless. If you buy trees or bushes from a far southern state, purchase in the spring or place the stock in storage during the first winter. A good storage place is one offering shelter from the cold with room to set the stock upright with roots covered by a mulch of straw and kept moist by occasional wetting. Another disadvantage of southern-grown trees is variation in the season. Trees in the south do not become dormant until much later than those in the north. Also the dormant season is shorter. Trees purchased in autumn may be shipped too late as to encounter very cold weather in the shipping, yet they should be in the dormant stage. I have decided late November is the ideal time for shipment to the north. If one waits until spring, stock from the south may well be in partial leafage when it arrives. Trees have an inner strength to push out leaves and then additional roots in springtime planting. When leaves develop prior to being planted, their ability to survive and grow is diminished. Southern-bought trees can fall into that category.

By the same rule, buyers be aware of trees being sold locally that are bare rooted and already in leaf, those being sold at discount late in the planting season, those offered by mail by one-time out-of-state advertisers.

Directions Given to Customers

A balled tree is simply a tree with a portion of its root still attached to the soil in which it was growing. The ball of earth is wrapped with a strong but inexpensive material called burlap. It will decay rapidly under earth due to dampness. Do not remove it when planting the tree. Do not remove the nails that pin the burlap. Handle the ball carefully.

All balled trees, whether they be evergreen or deciduous, are planted the same way. Dig the hole slightly larger in diameter and three to four inches deeper than the diameter and depth of the ball to be planted. Return about one third of the removed soil to the hole. Be sure it is well pulverized and free of sizable stone, etc. Add a five-gallon pail of peat moss, moderately packed, and add clean water to produce a thick solution when all three are mixed. Determine which side of the tree goes in which direction and set it in the hole. Press it downward until the top of the ball is level to the ground surface. Do not lower the ball to below ground level. Do not plant trees in depressions that have no drainage. Do not plant trees in a drainage area between properties. Do not plant in the drainage area of roof drains. Too much water can cause a tree to die more quickly than can too dry a soil. After the tree ball has absorbed water from the planting hole, add more soil to fill all cavities and mound it up over the burlap to a depth not exceeding three to four inches. The extra soil will help retain moisture and help support the tree. Trees five feet tall and under need not be staked except in very windy areas. Evergreens taller than five feet and deciduous trees taller than eight feet should be staked. Staking means driving three secure stakes, in triangular fashion, into the ground just beyond the dug hole. Six- to eight-inch lengths of rubber hose are placed approximately four to six feet high in the tree, circled around the trunk just above supporting branches,and wire strung through each one and loosely secured. Loosely secured means do not tighten the wire loop around the tree but make certain it will not come undone. The opposite end is led to the stake and also would tightly. By driving individual stakes deeper the wire can be made tight, but not taut. Leave the stakes in for one full growing season, if the tree is small, two years if large, and three years if very large.

Do not fertilize trees planted in autumn. Fertilizing such trees is done in early spring, late March or early April, with the second application in June. Do not over-fertilize. One cup full of basic fertilizer, 10-10-10, or half that amount of 20-20-20 can be added to the planting mixture in spring planting or scattered around the ground surface in trees planted the previous autumn.

Water newly-planted trees weekly by wetting ground and foliage for about two minutes. Trees planted in gravel or sand need more precise watering than trees planted in clay mixed soils. Do not place lawn sprinklers near trees for watering purposes. Overwatering is just as injurious as underwatering.

Successful planting is the result of careful planting.

The Living Christmas Tree

The majority of so-called living Christmas trees are trees that are dug and burlapped similar to those being planted in lawns. The one difference is that live Christmas trees must be dug prior to winter ground freeze and, consequently, be stored for a time until retailed. The roots of most evergreens extend far beyond the outer branches of the tree and must be cut off in the process of being dug. The larger the tree the greater percentage of root must be severed. Such a tree planted immediately in a suitable soil is more likely to survive than if it is stored for a period of time, then kept for days in a warm house, then shocked by being thrust out into the cold of winter. Do not be discouraged by this warning. Living Christmas trees serve a dual purpose and with care can be a successful undertaking. Keep the tree in the house seven days or less – the shorter the time the better. Place the ball of earth in a container, a strong cardboard box, or nested in an automobile tire. Line the containing unit with plastic so that a cupful of water can be added daily to the soil for continued moisture. If bulbs are placed on the tree position them over limbs rather than underneath. Keep the tree as far distant from hot air registers as is practical. If the temperature is below freezing when the tree is taken from the house, place it in a garage or other building until a warming trend sets in. If conditions are right it can then be planted, especially if the hole was dug prior to ground freezing and the soil kept under cover. If planting is too difficult place the tree in a protected area where snow and rainfall can fall on the foliage and plant it as early in spring as is possible. It should then be cared for as is a tree for general landscaping.

Care of White Birch Trees

The most commonly used birches in landscaping are Gray, European, Paper, and Weeping.

Gray Birch is a misleading name, as it tends to describe the Gray as being gray when it is white. All birch start out as dark brown saplings with short segments of line horizontally criss-crossing the trunk. Gray is a lowland birch, therefore shallow rooted and fast growing. At about a six-foot height the lower section starts to whiten and as the tree grows the white moves upward. It is smooth for the first few years, then becomes rough with diamond-shaped markings at the base, which like the whiteness, slowly moves upward as the tree ages. Gray can grow as rapidly as four to six feet per season in rich, moist soil. It is one of the birches that will grow in standing water if drainage takes place within days. It lends itself to clumping readily, sending out several shoots when the main one is severed. I explained this process in the description of birches in my general outline. Gray grows to about twenty-five feet with a fifteen-foot spread of branching. The leaf is small, about one inch in length, and turns bright yellow when autumn approaches. Some are cut-leaf type which means the edges of the leaves have sawtooth points and a crisp appearance resembling Ivy.

European grows fifty to sixty feet with a spread of about twenty feet. It, too, grows rapidly, and being a larger tree has a longer lifespan than the Gray. The bark on this tree requires several years to gain its whiteness, the white being very white and smooth to the touch. Roots are shallow, leaves are three to four inches in length, and the autumn color is yellow. It grows best in rich, well-drained soils.

Paper is a tall slender birch that, because of its height, grows best in protected areas. It is an upland type requiring well-drained soil. It is the whitest.

Premature Death of Trees

Those of us who are in the business of growing trees are concerned about trees that die before their time. Anyone walking through a woods of American Beech, or in wetter areas where White Ash are growing, are aware that trees are suffering and dying. Even more evident are White Birch in various stages of growth in landscaped areas. Because of questions often asked as to the reasons why, I wrote to the New York State Department of Environmental Conserva- tion. John Dupont of that department asked Michael J. Birmingham, Associate Forester, to reply and the following is based on information he wrote to me.

White Ash die from a disease known as ash yellows. It is due to a microplasma-like body which is a bacterium without a cell wall. The disease is not new, although actual knowledge has come only in the past ten years.

The Lombardy Poplar is dying from a disease known as bothichiza canker. This is a fungus that kills by girdling the trees. It gains entry through wounds. Trees suffering from insufficient watering and other deficiencies are particularly susceptible.

American Beech are dying from rot of interior core wood, a slow but constant deterioration that leaves mature trees with hollow centers. The cause is a disease known as fomes igniarius.

Sycamore Maples show spring damage because of winter injury to buds. It is due primarily to too low a temperature in mid-winter. Most recover the following spring and summer.

Maple demise, a term heard often, is not an accurate statement, according to Mr. Birmingham. Maples are not declining either in numbers nor in health. The major causes of disease in Sugars are old age, injury from heavy equipment both along roadsides and in the construction of housing, by the tapping for syrup, by changes in water drainage creating too wet a condition, and by insect defoliation. He claims that salt used to subdue winter ice, exhaust from vehicles, and contaminated air from other sources all contribute to a degree.

White Birch is a very popular tree that needs a more extensive explanation. Observations come to those who work with trees, and I have grown birch for many years. My nursery was originally surrounded by country. My first source of birch seedlings was due to an agreement with a neighbor. I became aware that the seedlings I was digging came from seed produced several years earlier. They appeared healthy, as did new growth shooting upward from stumps of trees that had succumbed to a disease that had destroyed both trunks and foliage but had not completely killed the trees. The seedlings continued to grow with no sign of the problem that had almost destroyed the parent trees.

I controlled unwanted bush and weed growth in my uncultivated nursery by spraying each unwanted growth with a herbicide. I soon learned that if the spray fell on the ground surface above birch roots the birch would die. I only had to contaminate a small portion of the root to lose the entire tree. I discontinued spraying herbicides near birch and in the past thirty years can count on the fingers of one hand the number of birch that have died in my nursery. I suspect that the use of herbicides affect adversely all trees, and shallow-rooted trees such as birch in particular. I know also that newly-planted trees of all varieties suffer when herbicides are applied to lawns.

According to Mr. Birmingham, birch need cool moist conditions. Most lawn areas are too hot and too dry during the summer and autumn months. Borers discovered in diseased trees and blamed for the death of the trees, is in error. Healthy birch grow faster to repair than borers can damage. Borers found in dead trees are there simply because the trees have not, for any one of several reasons, made sufficient growth to remain healthy.

Birch, like maples, have adapted to different soil conditions. Gray Birch grow best in wet to moist soils. Their lifespan is about twenty years. European lives twice that long and like medium moist but not too wet a soil. This variety begins to whiten at the base when the tree reaches about ten feet in height. Paper Birch likes dry soils. This slender tree grows tall, lives long, and has the whitest bark of all the birches.

Soil—What Exactly Is It?

It is only fitting that this book contain some information about soil. Many home purchasers are unaware of the importance of good soil surrounding the house. It is not a prime topic when one is considering construction, plumbing, heating, access to electrical outlets, and the numerous additional items that must be given close scrutiny. What lies beneath the new grass growing in the front lawn is taken for granted. What kind of soil lies there is dependent on so many different factors. Was the house built on existing land? Or was the land constructed along with the building by having it trucked in to fill swamp land, or gravel bed, or a past dump site? Did the builder realize the importance of the top few inches in and around the house, carefully removing it while in the building process and replacing it when the building was complete? Did he take care not to mix it with subsoil? Or did he truck it off to another location with the intent of robbing this homeowner to satisfy another one? Regardless of whether the answers are yes or no, the packing down of soil by heavy equipment in the process of leveling off and grading for lawn does damage. It is damage that the homeowner must endure if he or she has difficulty in digging adequate sized holes and encouraging plants to grow. We cannot easily change building methods but we can become more enlightened regarding soil. Just what is soil?

Soil is a composite of many things. Clay is fine particles of pulverized rock that, by itself, does not make a good growing soil as it is too dense for roots to penetrate. Gravel is small stone in various sizes left behind after flowing water washed out clay and other lighter materials. It, too, is not by itself conducive to the growth of plants. Humus is a brown, or dark-colored, soil formed by the decay of grasses and plants and those include trees. The name given to this soil in pure form is muck. Muck can become very dry, can burn in this stage if ignited, can blow from the source in strong wind. Muck is ideal for the growth of most living plants. The amount of muck mixed with either clay or gravel determines the grade of the mixture for good growing conditions. We add peat to soil when planting to give it a greater percentage of humus to the inert materials. The amount to be used is at the discretion of the person doing the planting but it can never be too much. I usually recommend a minimum of a five-gallon pail of moderately packed peat per single tree planting, somewhat less for smaller shrubs and double that amount for large trees.

Growing plants need chemicals just as humans do. These must be added to the soil for good plant growth. We call this replacement a fertilizer. Fertilizer is a balance of chemicals mixed with an inert material so it can be distributed more evenly. That material is often ground-up oyster shell or bone from slaughter houses. The amount of chemical mixed is designated by a series of numbers. Thus a 5-10-5 analysis would contain five pounds of nitrogen, ten pounds of phosphorus and five pounds of potassium per 100 pounds of the total. A 10-20-10 analysis has twice the amount of chemical as the former. The amount applied should always be in relation to the strength of the mixture. Testing indicates that one cupful of a basic 10-10-10 is the maximum that should be used in planting the average sized tree, evergreen or deciduous. By average I refer to a two-inch caliper by approximately ten to twelve feet tall for deciduous trees and six feet or less for evergreens. Smaller plantings should have smaller amounts and larger plantings proportionally more but within reason. Just as too much water can kill a tree, too much fertilizer can also kill. The chemicals contribute to leaf, stem and root growth. Other chemicals are also included and usually stated so in smaller print.

In this day and age of labor saving devices, fertilizers are not excepted. There are "weed and feed" types that do two jobs with a single application. The two do not always need to be done and, naturally, should never be used in plantings of any kind. Also advertized are fertilizer spikes. Drive several into the ground in the vicinity of the tree to be fertilized and think no more about it. Unfortunately spikes require moisture for leaching adequate chemical into the soil.

If the summer is dry and manual watering neglected the fertilizing takes place in autumn rains which is the wrong time of year. Fertilizing in autumn encourages bud growth which then can be harmed by winter's cold temperatures. Exception are grasses which usually have a cover of snow. Most lawns need no autumn fertilizing. The ones that do are those newly established, those injured by the chafer grub, or those beneath large shade trees. Purchase a large sieve and sift fertilizer only on those areas that appear to need it. Wash the sieve clean after each application to prevent rusting. A sieve can also be used to apply pesticide. Use caution, a nose mask and protective gloves when using pesticides in any form.

In discussing herbicides and pesticides do not be confused. Herbicides, or weed killers being the term more often, kill plants. Growing trees that are rooted deeply can survive the application of a herbicide to the surface area but more shallow rooted plants suffer. White Birch is especially susceptible to injury. A pesticide is not harmful to trees, shrubs, or grass. It is necessary to apply a pesticide to control two destructive pests, clinch bugs and chafer grubs. Both are controlled with a single application.

The chafer grub was reportedly brought into Newark, New York by entry of soil-bearing bushes from Europe. It gained a toehold to multiply and advance outward in ever widening circles. When that circle reached Marion, a town eight miles from Newark, New York State set up a program to contain the insect, but it failed and after several years it was abandoned. The bug itself is harmless, dying soon after laying eggs. The eggs are deposited in grassy areas, sometimes under and near the trees where mating took place. If you look upward against the background of sky on warm summer evenings and see numerous bugs flying in and around treetops you can be almost certain of damage to your lawn shortly after. (Do not confuse chafers with June bugs, which are much larger.) The eggs hatch into white grubs with brown heads. They feed on grass roots, destroying the grass so that it withers and dies. If deposited eggs are in close proximity whole areas of lawn can be made bare. Control is pesticide application in late August or early September before excessive damage is done. Most garden stores carry the granular pesticide needed. It is applied prior to rain or watered by garden hose to penetrate the surface soil. Select a windless day. Use a face mask and wear gloves. Remain off the treated area for one full day after treatment.

Landscaping a Home

Landscaping a home is the placement of shrubs and trees to enhance the house, and at the same time, please the owner. Properly landscaped lawns increase property value. Planted trees become part of capital investment and cannot, legally, be dug to be removed if the property is sold, unless of course by agreement with the purchaser. All such additions to capital investment should be documented and those documents placed in a secure safety box.

Large nurseries, with the intent in mind to increase business, send salesmen to owners of new homes to sell not only a plan for landscaping, but the trees and shrubbery to fill that plan. The salesman must not only be efficient in knowledge about the plants he is selling but about the soil surrounding the house. The right tree in the right type of soil can become a tree of beauty. The right tree in the improper soil may live, may even grow, but it will never obtain its full potential. Homeowners who are surprised by the poor quality of soil in lawn areas must exercise special care in planting. It is not necessary to dig a deep hole for a tree because nutrients come from near-surface soil. Dig the hole only inches deeper than normal but with added width. Use generous amounts of peat moss and mix it well with the soil when returning soil to refill the hole. Refrain from planting flowers, etc., around newly planted trees. The replaced soil should not be disturbed until the tree becomes established.

Those who decide to do their own planning and planting can obtain help at local libraries. Just as this book may someday be obtainable at a library so are books by others specializing in lawn design and landscaping. Keep in mind that trees are not in the same category as garden plants. They can grow to tremendous size and can interfere with each other or with the house itself. Place a schematic of the area to be landscaped on a flat surface and draw realistic circles of trees at maturity. Try not to overlap the circles. You may be surprised at the distances you are to maintain if you follow this suggestion.

In many years of delivery and conversation with customers regarding possible sites for various trees I pass on the following. Check evergreen trees closely before planting. One side is usually better than the other. Place a marking on that side so you will know which way to face the tree to its best advantage. Keep in mind that the south side, the sunlit side, outgrows the north side. If the tree has a less attractive side, turn that side southward. In a space of three or four years' time it will vastly improve.

The placing of evergreens, because of size and density, requires consideration. Some homeowners need to check overhead transmission lines to avoid drastic pruning of trees in the future. The drift of salt spray in winter can be a problem. A safe distance from the edge of the road to the tree site is about nine feet on homes fronting east-west roads. If roads are in thirty-mile-per-hour speed areas, perhaps six feet from the culvert is safe. Those living on north-south roads with high-speed traffic should maintain the nine-foot distance on the west side and increased it to twelve feet on the east side. Covering, in the form of heavy grade burlap or plastic sheeting, can add to protection. Do not enclose the tree tightly in plastic sheeting as heat from the sun can kill the tree.

I repeat the warning not to plant evergreens in low spots in lawns, in water runoff ditches between properties, or in the path of drainage from roof drains. Just keep in mind that too much watering can kill as quickly as too little watering, maybe even more quickly.

Epidemic Plant Diseases

Plants are an extension of the human race. Keeping that in mind tells us that plants are subject to the same kind of invasion by germs, viruses, bacteria, fungi, cankor as are humans, and in addition, insects. We, fortunately, have professionals who help us rid ourselves of chronic disease; plants have to go it alone. Walk into any woods and stand for a moment to scrutinize the trees for disease. It is everywhere. Isn't it fortunate it is suffered in silence? What we have to remind ourselves of is that the world has been around a long time. The one who regulates nature takes care that the balance is maintained. We can assist if we understand the problem. At the present time the old standby Elm is about done in by the elm beetle. This insect bores through the bark to feed upon and destroy the cambium layer. The cambium layer, to a plant, is similar to arteries and veins in a human. Injure it severely and the plant dies.

Just as bee stings can kill a human so can insects feeding on plant material kill the plant. In Blue Spruce it's the mites, sometimes called red spider. That is because they feed on the juices, comparable to blood in humans. Insects that feed on foliage seldom kill the host plant, because the feeding only destroys a portion of that available. If the portion consumed is great, such as the gypsy moth does, the host tree can be severely injured, possibly fatally. Nature usually corrects her mistakes. In 1985 the trumpet worm in maples had a banner year. This fast-moving worm protects itself doubly, first by constructing a tapered home with easy access, then folding the leaf downward over the house and holding it closed with an adhesive it secretes. No way could this pest be controlled by sprays. Traveling northward through New York State and into Canada, I was able to see infestation covering hundreds of miles. I felt saddened to think of the following year and years to come. But nature intervened. 1986 came with no repeat of the infestation, as did '87.

In 1984 or 1985, I forget which, maple trees lining the streets in towns and cities in New York State became infested with aphids. These sucking insects can be controlled by spraying. The time was late in September. The immediate problem was droplets from the sucking insects that fell on cars parked under the trees and on people passing back and forth. Those with spraying services available suggested spraying. Those concerned with costs procrastinated. Within a week's time heavy frost came to solve the dilemma. Both the leaves and insects were done in by nature's hand. I must add, however, not all epidemics are solved as easily or quickly as these two.

To the observing eye the health of plants becomes apparent in early autumn. Sickly trees, injured trees and old trees all show premature coloring of foliage. Now is the time to look more closely at foliage of fruit trees to see whether mice are girdling roots below ground level. Or to examine bark more closely at ground level on a tree with pre-coloring on one side while other foliage remains green. Determination can be made as to whether such a tree can be helped or not helped, or is simply the result of age. Some of the trees that are beyond help are American Chestnut, destroyed by a blight twenty to thirty years ago, and Beech, being currently attacked by a disease that destroys supporting wood to leave them hollow in the center. Lombardy Poplar is succumbing to a disease that kills quickly, Ash to a killer of unknown origin, Sycamore Maple to a virus that destroys leafing buds, and all maples are now in stage called maple demise. Whether that is due to air pollution, or acid rain, or some other cause is undetermined as yet. That the growing of healthy trees is becoming increasingly difficult is all the more reason to know your trees and their needs better. My hope is that this book will assist you.

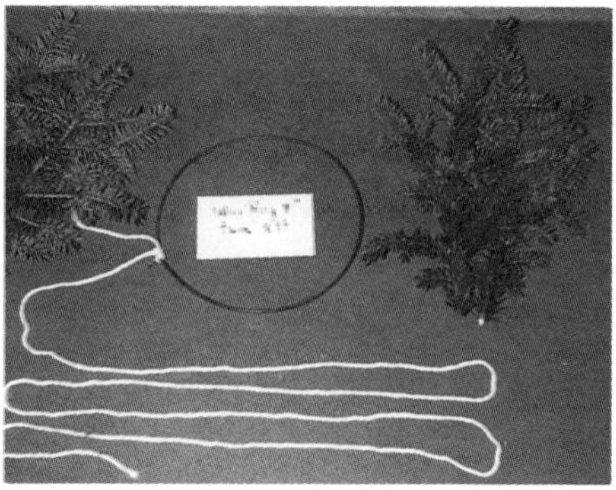

Ring is formed from number nine wire. Ends are twisted to interlock. Diameter is nine inches for a twenty-four inch wreath. Cord is strong twine approximately eight feet in length. Branches are Blue Spruce about eight inches in length.

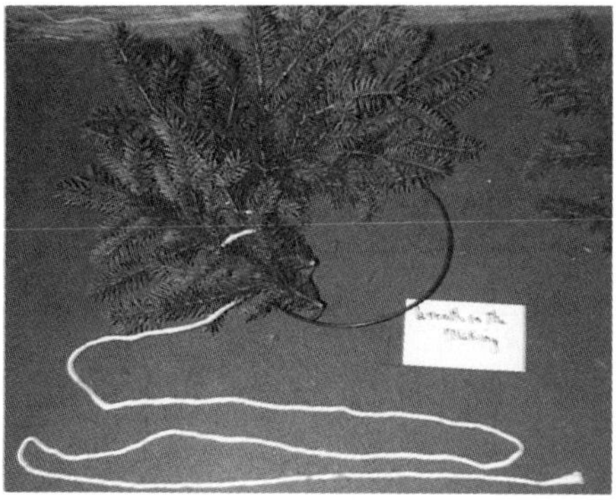

Partly-finished wreath showing angle of branches and method of securing them to the ring.

Finished wreath with my own special method of decorating. Silver and gold granular glitter is attached to the cones by spray glue.

Making a Christmas Wreath

I'd like to give directions for making a Christmas wreath. Branches of both pines and spruces can be used independently or together. I use only branch ends from blue spruce. Cut end branches in about twelve-inch lengths. Select those with balance and pointed tips. A small armful can make one wreath. Wear cloth gloves to protect hands and work on a mild day to make the task a pleasant one. Materials are sufficient boughs, cones for decoration, three-inch-wide red plastic ribbon, small flexible wire for the ties, a strong cord about seven feet in length, and a wire ring about ten inches in diameter. I use number nine grape wire for the ring.

Tie one end of the cord tightly to the ring and place the ring on a flat surface to be the work table. Place one branch at mid-point across the place of the tie, with the tips at a forty-five-degree angle outward. Wrap the cord over and around the branch to pull it tight and hold with the thumb of one hand. Place the second branch just behind the first so it covers the exposed cord, and again secure it. Continue until the wreath is complete. Tie the remaining end of the cord to the metal ring so it is secure. A ten-inch ring will suffice for a twenty-four-inch diameter wreath. Use a larger diameter ring for a larger wreath.

Cut the tie wire into twenty-four-inch lengths. Holding one cone firmly in one hand, wrap the wire around the base end pulling it down tightly into and between the seed cups. Allow about five inches of free wire for wrapping around the wreath. Place a second cone close to the first one and wrap the wire around that also. If the cones are not too large a third can be added to the string. The string of cones is placed across the face of the wreath, the ends of wire circling it to be twisted tightly. Three cone strings distanced evenly are sufficient for twenty-four-inch wreath. Cut the ribbon into ten-inch lengths. Lay them on a flat surface and slit the ends into three strips, using care to leave the mid-section of the ribbon intact. Lay the ribbon between the cone strings and parallel to the wreath, secure with a single strand of wire across the center and pulled tightly. This too is made secure by twisting. Add two more to complete the wreath decoration. Sparkle on cones can be added by wetting cones with pressurized glue and dusting with glitter immediately. A bow can be added if desired, or you can make use of artistic ability in other ways.

Reminders

A tree that grows best in wet soil can be safely planted in dry soil. However a tree that grows best in dry soil will die if planted in too wet a soil.

Autumn foliage coloring is due to exposure of colors screened by the deeper green of chlorophyll. Light frosts in autumn prohibit the production of additional chlorophyll while that already present is slowly absorbed back into the tree to reveal existing colors. Colors are enhanced by a good growing season followed by a series of light frosts.

Evergreens become dormant around mid-September. Time can vary from north to south. Dormancy remains until the new growth in spring reaches less than one inch length in growth. Deciduous trees become dormant when leaves drop from branching to remain so until new leaves show green in the spring. Both types can be dug and transplanted at any time during the dormant season.

Newly-planted trees need to be watered weekly during the first season, especially during the drier months of August and September. Stake evergreens taller than five feet and deciduous trees taller than eight feet. Staking should remain one year for small trees, and two years or longer for large trees.

Exposure of coloring in trees suggests some kind of injury if leaves turn prior to the autumn season. Reasons can be varied: too wet a soil for dry land trees, damage by mice to bark or roots, a herbicide applied too closely to the root area, roots damaged by cutting due to heavy machinery. In my opinion roots extending north, south, east, and west, sustain the north, south, east, and west above-ground branching. Also all can contribute to the whole tree. Thus a root can usually be severed without too much damage to the growing tree. But, not knowing the structure of underground roots, the removal of a sizable root cannot be assumed to not damage a tree.

Having grown trees for forty years, I can safely make the assertion that root pruning is not essential to tree survival. I might amend that to say that in certain type soils it might be necessary. Root pruning is the cutting off of roots that normally are cut in digging a tree but keeping the tree in its present location. Thus a tree is encouraged to grow new roots to replace those severed. A root pruned tree starts out faster and grows more quickly than one unpruned. However labor costs to prune, plus additional time in the nursery, contribute to a higher selling price. Some light-textured soils might require root pruning for trees to survive but the proper type soils make root pruning unnecessary. Proper soils are those with sufficient humus to cause particles to cling together. They must be relatively free of stone and must contain sufficient moisture to aid in the digging.

Questions concerning animal repellents can only be given general answers. Woodchucks can be destroyed by chemicals purchased at garden stores, poisons that are inserted into holes after which the openings are sealed. Raccoons can be trapped in cages to be, if the law permits, transported to areas distant from normal traveling routes. Deer are repelled by highly scented soaps placed in cloth and tied to bushes, by meat scraps from a butcher shop, human hair from a barber shop, and by moving objects such as cloth strips that move in strong winds. Cats and dogs can be discouraged by spray scents made for that purpose. Boundry, made by a company in New Jersey, is one that comes to mind. There may be others also.